WORDS ON THE PAGE, THE WORLD IN YOUR HANDS

BOOK THREE

Edited by
CATHERINE LIPKIN
and
VIRGINIA SOLOTAROFF

WORDS ON THE PAGE, THE WORLD IN YOUR HANDS

Prose and poetry written, selected, and adapted by contemporary writers for adults in literacy programs and others who wish to expand their reading horizons

PERENNIAL LIBRARY

HARPER & ROW, PUBLISHERS, NEW YORK
GRAND RAPIDS, PHILADELPHIA, ST. LOUIS, SAN FRANCISCO
LONDON, SINGAPORE, SYDNEY, TOKYO, TORONTO

To receive the complimentary teaching manual for *Words on the Page, The World in Your Hands,* please write to Department 361, Harper & Row, Publishers, 10 East 53rd Street, New York, NY 10022.

Grateful acknowledgment is made to Thomas M. Disch for the suggestion for the title *Words on the Page, The World in Your Hands.*

Copyright acknowledgments begin on p. 183.

FIRST EDITION

Designed by Barbara DuPree Knowles

LIBRARY OF CONGRESS CATALOGING-IN-PUBLICATION DATA

Words on the page, the world in your hands/Catherine Lipkin &
Virginia Solotaroff, eds.
    p. cm.
    ISBN 0-06-055154-2 (v. 1)   ISBN 0-06-096367-0 (pbk.: v. 1)
    ISBN 0-06-055155-0 (v. 2)   ISBN 0-06-096368-9 (pbk.: v. 2)
    ISBN 0-06-055156-9 (v. 3)   ISBN 0-06-096369-7 (pbk.: v. 3)
    1. Readers for new literates. 2. American literature—20th
century. I. Lipkin, Catherine. II. Solotaroff, Virginia.
PE1126.A4W6   1990
428.6'2—dc19   88-45952

90 91 92 93 94 CC/FG 10 9 8 7 6 5 4 3 2 1
90 91 92 93 94 CC/FG 10 9 8 7 6 5 4 3 2 1 (pbk.)

CONTENTS

Contents   vii

Contents   ix

Contents   xi

Contents

INTRODUCTION

José Garcia, a construction worker in his early thirties, came into a basic literacy program almost visibly trailing his shame. "I'm dumb," he said, without looking up. "I can't write." Neither could he read—in English or in Spanish, his native tongue—though he knew the alphabet, could print well, and his daughter, an alert second-grader, had started coaching him to read. He was, in fact, intelligent and ambitious, willing to come to an evening class following a workday that began at six in the morning.

At their first meeting, his tutor recorded the names of his work tools and his account of the tasks he performed with each of them. He was able to read these brief paragraphs. In meetings that followed, he spoke about his family and his school experience and was able to read an "autobiography" written in the words he had used to tell his story. His speaking vocabulary was becoming his reading vocabulary. He could soon read a simple story and, if it was in some way meaningful to him, learn its new words.

He was unable, however, to read and remember lists of unrelated vocabulary words—they meant nothing to him. And he was unwilling to read primers—"Run, Ken, run fast. You saw Igor take the money. Now he will kill you." José was studying on tired time and had a pressing need to learn about the real world. He had no patience for material he felt was trivial or meaningless.

The day he came in, tossed the "thriller" on the library table, and said, "I'm giving this back to you," was Martin Luther King's birthday. Copies of "I Have a Dream" had been set out on the table. José chose King's speech to replace the story of a boy who captured a thief as the text for the evening's lesson.

His tutor read "I Have a Dream" aloud. She and José discussed its themes, and together they found and underlined its many rhythmic repetitions. As they went through the piece again, José was responsible for reading the refrains. They read it a third time, in unison. Then José (with minor promptings) read the speech by himself, although it was well above his designated "grade" level. He was reading and understanding real writing! The splasher was suddenly swimming, and he knew it. For the first time he looked directly at his tutor and thanked her for the lesson. And he took King's speech home to read to his wife and daughter.

That experience set our minds in motion by highlighting a serious problem we shared with other literacy teachers. We had very little reading material to offer our students that in any way matched the seriousness of their commitment to learn—not only to identify the words on a page, that essential beginning, but to relate those words to the concerns of their lives.

Jonathan Kozel wrote *Illiterate America* in 1985. By juxtaposing the two words of his title for, perhaps, the first time, he alerted the informed public to a looming national crisis. He told us that twenty-five million American adults could not read product identification labels, menus, or street signs, and that an additional thirty-five million read "only at a level which is less than equal to the full survival needs of our society." "Together," he wrote, "these 60 million people represent more than one third of the entire adult population."

Certainly, underdeveloped reading skills are a severe vocational handicap. Just as surely, they impoverish the lives of those individuals who are thereby denied access to the information on which considered personal choices can be made. In recent years, as the social and human costs of illiteracy have come to light, government, industry, and trade unions have undertaken massive literacy programs. Their efforts have been constrained, however, by a scarcity of appropriate texts.

With few exceptions, the materials available for these programs have been written for children or have been developed by educators who, assuming that adults learn much as children do, emphasize phonics and word recognition, often at the expense of meaningful content. There is little juice or joy in a story written to incorporate a vocabulary list calibrated to early grade-level expectations. If literacy students are to experience the stimulation of thought and feeling and the strengthening of a sense of place in the human community that mature writing can engender, the texts they read must engage their adult imaginations and offer them opportunities to experience their surroundings in new ways.

How were we to provide such generative texts? We combed the literature, as others had done, and found only a handful of accessible poems and short prose passages and almost no extended work that was free of sophisticated reference, complex syntax, rare usage, or vocabulary that was well beyond the reach of inexperienced readers.

Having failed to find the texts we needed, we decided to write them ourselves. Guided by our good intentions, like others before us, we did so. We are okay writers, not good writers. We wrote okay stories, not good stories. Not good enough. Effort, pedagogical sensibility, and the best will in the world were no substitute for literary gift.

We decided to contact serious writers, several hundred of them, and ask for help. Their support for the project overwhelmed us. They responded to our suggestions, offered some of their own, and spread the word at writers' conferences. Those whose work did not lend itself to our needs suggested the names of colleagues we might contact. We are grateful to all of them. Through their generous efforts we have been able to gather the texts we wanted—good stories and poems that, in their fidelity to the ambiguity and truth of lived lives, reach out with their strange yet somehow familiar burdens. In weighted moments of recognition (for who has not lived through some version of the conflict, betrayal, innocence, joy, and despair these works contain?), they offer something we know in part, and lead us to reexamine related aspects of our own lives. Literature invites a response. In formulating that response, perceptions are sharpened, sympathies are widened, thoughts are clarified. Learning takes place.

Rather than "writing down" to their readers, the distinguished authors in the Harper & Row collections have written *to* them. Some have selected pieces from their published works, some have created original work, and others, by judicious adaptation, have made their work more widely accessible without sacrificing flavor, point, or power. One can say, then, that *Words on the Page, The World in Your Hands* represents the literary community reaching out to the literacy community by offering memorable stories, poems, and essays that challenge, enlighten, and delight.

The Editors

WORDS ON THE PAGE, THE WORLD IN YOUR HANDS

BOOK THREE

A TIME TO MOURN
*Adapted by Etheridge Knight
from his story "A Time to Mourn"*

He stepped out of the darkness and noise of the prison tag shop into a sea of sunshine washing the asphalt street and the industry buildings in a sheet of heat. He pulled his cap down over his eyes and followed the deputy warden's messenger down a spotless sidewalk that cut a path through the neatly mowed lawn, which lay like a green carpet dotted with great round flower beds and whirring lawn sprinklers.

He heard lazy shouts floating in the oppressive air and the sharp smack of a baseball being slammed. To his left he saw a few men shagging flies out on the field. The bare dirt diamond looked like an open palm against the green carpet. Above the outfield, on top of the wall, he saw a guard watching the players, squatting on his heels, his rifle across his lap.

He followed the warden's messenger past the wire-enclosed brick powerhouse. Its twin smokestacks, piercing the sky like devil's horns, dominated the entire prison. He nodded to the group of men working on the coal piled against the powerhouse, and one of them called out: "What's up, Big Joe?"

He ignored the question but shot a glance at the slick-haired messenger strutting ahead of him, swinging his arms and clicking his heels against the sidewalk. The same question rose in his own throat, but he swallowed it. He was Big Joe Noonan; he didn't ask for explanations from a swaggering little fink who worked for the deputy. He raised his cap, ran his hand over his kinky black hair, now speckled with gray, then settled the cap back on his head and lifted his chin. He was a lifer; he would wait and see.

When the buzzer sounded outside the deputy's office, he rose from the bench and walked over to the guard standing at the deputy's door. Turning his back and raising his arms, he stood silent as the guard's hands moved over him: under his arms, down the center of his back, over his buttocks, between his legs, and down to his socks. Then the guard tapped him lightly on the shoulder, and he turned and walked into the deputy's office.

His face remained unchanged when he saw the prison chaplain sitting behind the deputy's desk. He thought

So this is the pitch. "Why haven't you been in church lately, Joe?" Well, listen to his speech . . . smile nice . . . then go back to work.

He moved to the front of the desk and looked down into the bright eyes of the chaplain.

I'm here, Reverend Dickerson. No sweat. I'll listen.

No trouble. *Just rattle it off and let me get back to work.* Aloud he said, "You sent for me, sir?"

"Yes, Joe." The chaplain waved to a straight-backed chair. "I won't beat around the bush, Joe. I'm afraid I have some bad news for you. The warden received a telegram today that your uncle has died. As you know, it's my job to inform you men of such things. And I'm truly sorry, Joe. I see from your record here that your uncle is listed as your only living relative . . . ?"

His eyes dropped to the shiny desktop.

Dead . . . the old man dead. Ha! Dead as a fish. . . . Look out the window. . . . And my only living relative? What about my daughter that they gave away? She's twenty-two now, and I wouldn't know her if I saw her . . . and she wouldn't see me anyway. I killed her mother. . . . I-killed-her-mother, I-killed-her-mother. . . . Look out the window, no trouble. . . . *Uncle Jake dead . . . ?* No sweat, no trouble. Listen and go back to work.

He unfolded his arms and slowly rubbed his hands up and down his trouser legs. Then he folded them again across his chest.

"As you know, Joe, it is our policy to allow a man to attend the funeral of his immediate family—that is, if he can afford the expense for himself and, of course, for the guard to go with him."

Uncle Jake dead! I wonder if they shaved off his gray mustache too . . . I wonder if he wet the bed . . . I wonder if he was scared like I was scared

of the Chair and the smell of the Lysol . . . I killed
her mother, and they are dead. . . . Uncle Jake
and Marta are dead. . . .

"Since your uncle resided outside the state," the
chaplain went on, "that policy would not apply. However, you will be permitted to send a message of sympa-
thy, and flowers, if you like. . . ."

I should say something. I should . . . flowers I
should send the dead. Marta liked red ones and
yellow ones, red-and-yellow. . . . No sweat, no
trouble.

He kept his eyes on the shiny desktop and his arms
folded across his chest.

"I know this is hard news, Joe," the chaplain was
saying. "Perhaps you'd like to talk to me about your
uncle."

He shoved his chair back and stood up. "No, thank
you, sir," he said, "but I appreciate you letting me
know."

"I'm sorry, Joe."

"Thank you, sir," he said, turning to go.

"Oh yes, Joe, one more thing. If you want to, you
may be excused from work. You can go directly to your
cell. Perhaps you'd like to be by yourself for a while?"

"If it's all the same, sir, I'd like to go back to work."

He left the deputy's office and once more followed
the slick-haired messenger down the spotless sidewalk.
Uncle Jake dead and Marta dead. . . . A time to
mourn. And this slick-haired fink prancing in front

of me like a woman. Marta was a woman . . . and my
daughter. A time to mourn and a time to die, a
time to weep and a time to dance. . . . My Marta
danced, danced-and- danced with anybody . . . and
I wept, cried red blood. . . . Marta is dead, died
crying, and Jake is dead. No sweat . . . no trouble
. . . *and* . . .

He turned the corner by the powerhouse and
quickly stepped off the sidewalk. Four guards, their
white caps gleaming in the sun, were hustling a young
convict down the walk toward the deputy's office. As they
passed, Joe saw the young man's face lifted to the sky,
his black skin glistening with sweat, blood running from
a cut above his eye. His lips were pulled tightly from his
teeth as he struggled to free himself. Joe pressed his
back against the powerhouse fence, his fingers grasping
the wire mesh. He watched the five men scuffle by, silent
except for their hard breathing and the scraping of their
shoe soles on the concrete. His eyes locked with those
of the convict for an instant before the young man was
hustled around the corner and out of sight.

The convicts had come over from the coal pile and
lined up along the fence, their fingers hooked through
the wire.

"That kid's doin' hard time."

"Yeah, he's got a lot to learn."

"I bet he wear out 'fore the Hole do."

"Say, did you see that lump he put on ol' Fat
Ass . . ."

Joe fell into step behind the messenger, and the voices faded away.

Uncle Jake is dead and that kid is dead and has got a lot to learn . . . like Marta had a lot to learn. Yeah, I fought 'em, too, twenty years ago, and I died in the Hole, and the Hole is still there . . . and that kid is dead, red flowing from his head and Marta's chest. . . . Twenty years and the kid will learn that he is dead like Marta and me and Uncle Jake, dead weeping. . . . Slow down, kid, no sweat, no trouble.

"The chaplain told me about your uncle, Joe. Sure you don't want me to take you to the cellhouse?" They were at the door of the tag shop. The messenger turned around and leaned against the door and looked up at Joe with an unspoken question deep in his eyes. "Nobody's in the cellhouse now, Joe; it's quiet there and . . . everything. . . ."

"No, kid. No, thanks."

The slick-haired messenger threw up his hand and moved off. "Well, maybe sometime? See ya."

Joe stepped inside the dim tag shop, into the rhythmic pulsing of one hundred machines. After checking in with the plant guard, he went to his locker and hung up his cap; then he went to his stamping press and flipped the on switch. Settling himself on his stool, he picked up a stack of license plates and began to feed them, one by one, into the hungry machine. Into the right side, out the left. No sweat, no trouble.

TO EVERY THING THERE IS A SEASON

*From the Book of Ecclesiastes,
Chapter 3, Verses 1–8 and 11*

1   To every thing there is a season,
     and a time to every purpose under heaven:

2   A time to be born,
     and a time to die;
     a time to plant,
     and a time to pluck up that which has been planted;

3   A time to kill,
     and a time to heal;
     a time to break down,
     and a time to build up;

4   A time to weep,
     and a time to laugh;
     a time to mourn,
     and a time to dance;

5   A time to cast away stones,
     and a time to gather stones together;
     a time to embrace,
     and a time to refrain from embracing;

6 A time to get,
    and a time to loose;
    a time to keep,
    and a time to cast away;

7 A time to rend,
    and a time to sew;
    a time to keep silence
    and a time to speak;

8 A time to love,
    and a time to hate;
    a time of war,
    and a time of peace
    . . . .

11 He made everything beautiful
        in its time.

ENDURANCE IS THE ULTIMATE VIRTUE
◄§ Dennis Brutus

Endurance is the ultimate virtue
—more, the essential thread
on which existence is strung
when one is stripped to nothing else
and not to endure is to end in despair.

EVEN NIGHTINGALES
◄§ Dennis Brutus

Even nightingales
by West Lake cannot silence
the wail of exile.

THE TEMPTATION OF JESUS

*From the Book of Matthew, Chapter 4,
translated from the Greek by Morton Smith*

Then Jesus was driven by the Spirit into the barren land to be tempted by the Devil. And having fasted forty days and forty nights, afterwards, he was hungry.

And the tempter, coming, said to him, "If you are the Son of God, order that these stones become bread."

But Jesus, answering, said:

"It has been written, 'A man shall not live by bread alone, but by every word that comes out of the mouth of God.'"

Then the Devil took him into the holy city and stood him on the tip of the temple, and said to him:

"If you are the Son of God, throw yourself down, for it has been written, 'He will give his angels orders about you and they will hold you up on their hands so that you will not strike your foot against a stone.'"

Jesus said to him:

"It has also been written, 'You shall not tempt the Lord your God.'"

Again, the Devil took him into a very high mountain and showed him all the kingdoms of the world and their glory, and he said to him:

"I will give you all of these if you will kneel and subject yourself to me."

Then Jesus said to him:

"Be gone, Satan, for it has been written, 'You shall subject yourself to the Lord your God, and shall serve him alone.' "

Then the Devil left him and angels appeared, came near, and served him.

FIRST PRO FIGHT

*Adapted by Joyce Carol Oates
from her book* On Boxing

They are young welterweight boxers so equally matched they look like twins, though one has a red-head's pale skin and the other is a dark-skinned His-panic. They circle each other in the ring, under the bright lights, trying jabs, left hooks, and right crosses that turn weak in mid-air and become harmless slaps.

How to get inside! How to score a point or two! How to land a single real punch! The boys seem to have forgotten all they have been trained to do, and the Madi-son Square Garden fight crowd is getting noisy and angry. Time is running out.

"Those two—what did they do, wake up this morn-ing and decide they were boxers?" a man behind me says in disgust. He is well dressed, with a neat mustache and sunglasses. A real fight fan. Knows all the answers. Two hours later, during the main event, he will be screaming, "Tommy! Tommy! Tommy!" over and over when mid-dleweight champion Marvelous Marvin Hagler knocks out Thomas Hearns.

The young welterweights must hear the boos and catcalls in the Garden, but they are locked in their fight, circling each other, "dancing," jabbing, slapping—light

blows, bad footwork. Now one more clinch in the ropes makes the crowd yell.

Why are they here in the Garden of all places? Is each one fighting his first professional fight? They do not want to hurt each other. The bell rings at the end of the fourth and last round. The crowd yells louder.

The decision is announced—"A draw." The crowd gets more angry. "Get out of the ring!" "Go home!"

The Hispanic boy, in yellow shorts, with damp curly hair, walks around his corner of the ring with his hand raised—not to make people more angry but just to say, "I am here, I made it, I did it."

BOTTLE CAPS

~§ *Stuart Dybek*

Each day I'd collect caps from beer bottles. I'd go early in the morning through the alleys with a shopping bag, the way I'd seen old women and bums pick through trash in a cloud of flies. Collectors of all kinds hung out in the alleys: scrap collectors, bottle collectors, other people's hubcap collectors. I made my rounds, stopping behind bars, where bottle caps spilled from splitting bags still smelling of beer from the night before.

I'd hose them down and store them in coffee cans. At the end of the week, I'd line my bottle caps up for contests between the brands. It was basically a three-way race among Pabst with its blue-ribboned cap, Bud, and Miller's. Blatz and Schlitz weren't far behind.

That got boring fast. It was a rare bottle cap that kept me collecting—Carling's Black Label, with its matching black cap, or Monarch, from the brewery down the street, its gold caps like pieces of eight, and Meister Bräu Bock, my favorite, each cap a ram's-head medal.

By July, I had too many to count. The coffee cans hidden in the basement began to stink. I worried that my mother would find out. It would look to her like I was brewing a disease. Still, I collected and hoarded my bottle caps. Some were lined with cork, some with plastic, some with foil. I tapped the dents from those too badly mangled by openers. When friends asked for bottle caps to decorate the spokes on their bikes, I wouldn't give them any.

One afternoon I caught my younger brother in the basement, stuffing my bottle caps into his pocket.

"What do you think you're doing?" I demanded.

At first he wouldn't talk, but I had him by the T-shirt, which I worked up around his throat, slowly twisting it to a knot at his windpipe.

He led me into the backyard, to a sunless patch behind the oil shed, and pointed. Everywhere I looked I could see my bottle caps, half buried, their jagged edges sticking up among clothespin crosses and pieces of colored glass.

"I've been using them as tombstones," he said, "in my insect graveyard."

DIVERS

Robert Francis

Where the white water lilies float upon black water
Boys sleek and dripping as the stems of water lilies
Run and dive shallow from their tipping raft, their
    aim
Not to touch bottom when their white heels disap-
    pear.

But give them a deep pool paved with white
    sand and pebbles
Or cove of some blue mineral lake and watch
    them plunge
Straight down breathless, until a muskrat head
Bobs up and then a hand clutching the trophy
    sand.

THE AVOWAL
Denise Levertov

As swimmers dare
to lie face to the sky
and water bears them,
as hawks rest upon air
and air sustains them,
so would I learn to attain
freefall, and float
into Creator Spirit's deep embrace,
knowing no effort earns
that all-surrounding grace.

ENGRAVED

ᏋᏱ Denise Levertov

A man and a woman
sit by the riverbank.
He fishes,
she reads.
The fish are not biting.
She has not turned the page
for an hour.
The light around them
holds itself taut,
no shadow moves,
but the sky and the woods,
look, are dark.
Night has advanced upon them.

MIDSUMMER

❧ Robert Francis

Twelve white cattle on the crest,
Milk-white against the chicory skies,
Six gazing south, six gazing west
With the blue distance in their eyes.
Twelve white cattle standing still.
Why should they move? There are no flies
To tease them on this wind-washed hill.
Twelve white cattle utterly at rest.
Why should they graze? They are past grazing.
They have cropped the grass, they have had their
    fill.
Now they stand gazing, they stand gazing.
Only the tall redtop about their knees
And the white clouds above the hill
Move in the softly moving breeze.
The cattle move not, they are still.

THE COLONEL OF THE CIVIL GUARD

From the novel Don Juan *by Azorín*
(translated from the Spanish by Douglas Unger)

The best inn in the city is the little place called La Perla. The ground floor is a café; on the other floors are rooms, white and clean. Don Teodoro Moreno, colonel of the Civil Guard, chief of the security forces, has seated himself in the café; with him is Pozas.

The colonel lives in the inn, but he spends most of the day and part of the night in the café. There he reads the newspapers and writes his letters. Colonel Don Teodoro is a powerful man, large and heavy, with a long, full beard. His hands are strong and knotted. His soldiers idolized him. He never used weapons; he always carried a short cane in his hand. In the most horrible battles, when bullets flew all around, Don Teodoro would stop, look about him, take out a package of cigarette papers. He would rip out a paper and stick it to his lip. The bullets whistled past. Next, he would take out an old leather tobacco pouch and give it two little taps. He would open it and pour tobacco into his hand. Bombs exploded; bullets screamed. Don Teodoro would gently squeeze the tobacco with his other hand. He would roll a cigarette, light it, tilt his head up, and let out a heavy stream of smoke to the sky. . . .

"You were telling me, my dear Pozas," said the colonel, "that to maintain authority . . ."

"I was telling you," continued Pozas, "that to maintain one's authority—"

"Ruperto!" interrupted the colonel, calling for the waiter.

The waiter, silently, took away the empty dark beer that was sitting in front of Don Teodoro and brought him a full one.

The colonel ran his hand, gently, over his beard; his sad, wandering eyes looked out into the street.

"Pozas, do you see?" he said very suddenly. "That woman has the same way of walking as my poor Adela had. . . ."

At that moment the tragedy of Don Teodoro's life passed through his mind. One day his wife, nearing the time to deliver her third child, going about the house as usual, went to sit down in a chair, fell to the floor, aborted the child, and died. After that came the suicide of his son Pepe at the military academy: his son Pepe, so full of honor and intelligence. Then his other son, Antonito, twelve years old, fell from his bicycle, hit his head on a rock, and died in two hours.

"Ruperto!" shouted the colonel again.

The waiter, silently, served him another dark beer.

"You were saying, my dear Pozas, that to maintain authority . . ."

Suddenly a captain entered and crossed the café. He stopped in front of Don Teodoro, clicked his heels in military style, saluted, and said, "Colonel, sir, I have just arrived with the prisoners from Barcelona. . . ."

Don Teodoro slowly finished off the beer in front of him. Where the beer had sat, he put his elbow. Resting his head in his hand, he stared down at the marble tabletop. He sat this way for a moment in silence. Then he lifted his head and said, "How many are there?"

"Eight and a boy," the captain answered.

"A boy?" Don Teodoro asked.

"Yes, sir; a boy twelve or maybe thirteen years old."

The colonel leaned in silence for another moment over the table. Then he said, "Order them to bring the boy to me."

A short time later, a sergeant entered with the boy. He was a blond boy with lively blue eyes. His hair had not been cut for a long time. He wore a jacket too large for him, tied in the middle with a hemp rope. His toes stuck out through the holes in his shoes. He was covered with dust.

"What's your name?" Don Teodoro asked him.

"Marianet," said the boy.

"Marianet what?" asked Don Teodoro.

"Marianet Vargas," the boy said.

"What did you do in Barcelona?"

The boy didn't answer. He shrugged his shoulders; he shifted his head from side to side; he laughed.

"What have you done in Barcelona?" insisted the colonel.

"Nothing," he said finally. He lifted his hands. "I was out in the streets. . . ."

"Ruperto!" the colonel shouted. "Bring this boy a couple of ham sandwiches." At the same time he pointed to his own empty glass.

The boy sat down next to the colonel. The waiter brought what he was asked. As the boy wolfed the food down, the colonel drank slowly, with a look of deep sadness.

"You were saying, my dear Pozas, that the way to maintain authority . . ."

LIBERTY

W. S. Merwin

Every morning
somebody unlocks the statue
and lets in the day crew

first the welders who are fixing
the crack in the arm
that holds up the torch

and the elevator operators
the ticket sellers and the guides
and the next shift of police

the early ferries
land from the city
bringing visitors

born everywhere
to the cemented pedestal
under the huge toes

to follow signs
to the ticket booths
vendors conveniences

and to the guides to the crown and the arm
and the torch
whatever is safe

and the guides tell the names
of the sculptor and the donor
and explain why it is ours

also how much it weighs
and how many come to see it
in a year

and the name of the island
from which the foreigners
used to watch it

MYRTLE THE TURTLE P.S. 222

Peter Meinke

Because we always said "Toity-toid Street" and "Shut da daw," Miss Endicott made up an exercise for us so we could lose our accent and become President of the United States. But Bobby Pepitone said shit he din wanna be no president y'ever see a president chewin gum? nosir. But we had to do the exercise anyway. It was a poem called "Myrtle the Turtle." We were supposed to recite very clearly, "There once was a *turtle* whose *first* name was *Myrtle* swam out to the *Jersey shore,*" but of course we each got up in front of the class scratching ourselves and ducking spitballs and said, "Aah dere once wuz a toitle whose foist name wuz Moitle," while Miss Endicott tore her hair out. I just visited Bobby Pepitone, and to judge by the way his kids talk, poor Miss Endicott must be completely bald by now—"like a toitle," his kids would say.

AUNT GERTRUD

❧ *Peter Meinke*

My seven aunts never left Brooklyn,
but Aunt Gertrud read travel books so hard
she felt she had actually gone.

"The fish in Macedonia," she'd say,
"you vouldn't belief—they melt in your mouth
like cream cheese!" "And never," she warned her
   sisters,
their gray heads bobbing like barn owls,
"never stand alone on a corner in Naples!"

Her travels made her liberal, and when
some other aunt would lecture
about our ungodly hours, she'd stroke
my eager head and say, eyes round as rupees—
"Vell,
you're only young vunce, ain't you?"

THE CHILDREN

◆§ Peter Meinke

What did we children want?
The cherry from the cocktail,
the drumstick from the turkey.
To hear the aunts sing with Uncle Jim.
To smoke cigars and see the grownups naked.
To keep the turtle I brought back from Rockaway.
To stay up late and listen to the jokes.
To stay up late and listen to the arguments.

Our parents were people who got along with
    children
so we grew, unresentful, unrepressed,
more or less doing what we wanted.
And to the very end the turtle
made its steady rounds throughout the house,
exploring rooms and hallways all night long,
and banging in the corners as it turned,
like a ghost rattling the locked cupboard doors.

THE HEART'S LOCATION

Peter Meinke

All my plans for suicide are ridiculous.
I can never remember the heart's location.
Too cheap to smash a car,
too queasy to slash a wrist,
once jumped off a bridge and
almost scared myself to death
then spent two foggy weeks
waiting for new glasses.

Of course I really want to live,
continuing my lifelong search
for the world's greatest unknown cheap restaurant,
and a poem full of ordinary words
about simple things,
in the inconsolable rhythms of the heart.

A POEM ON THE DEATH OF THE MAN WHO INVENTED PLASTIC ROSES

Peter Meinke

The man who invented the plastic rose
is dead. Behold his mark:
his undying flawless blossoms never close
but guard his grave unbending through the dark.

He understood neither beauty nor flowers,
which catch our hearts in nets as soft as sky
and bind us in their web of fragile hours.
Flowers are beautiful because they die.

TEX ARKANA

*❧ Adapted from Richard Ford's
novel* A Piece of My Heart

In Jackson, Mississippi, in 1953, Sam's father brought him downtown and left him in the lobby of the King Edward Hotel while he went upstairs to talk to a man about selling starch.

Sam's mother was home in bed, too sick to watch him, so he sat there in the lobby waiting for his father. He watched the men standing around smoking cigars and shaking hands for minutes at a time. In a little while a midget came into the lobby wearing cowboy boots and a Texas hat, and attracted everyone's attention as he signed his name to the register. He gave the bellboy a tip before he ever touched a bag.

When he was ready to go to his room, the midget turned and looked all around the lobby, as if he were looking for someone to meet him. When he saw the boy sitting on the long couch, he came across in his midget's gait that made him look as if he were wearing diapers. He told the boy that his name was Tex Arkana and that he was in the movies. He had been the midget in *Samson and Delilah* and had been one of the Philistines that Samson had killed with the jawbone of a mule.

Sam said he had seen the movie and remembered

the midget fairly well. The midget told him that in his bags he had all his movie photos and a scrapbook with his newspaper clippings. He said he would be glad to show them to Sam, if he would care to see.

Most of the men in the lobby were watching the two of them sitting on the couch talking. When the boy said that he *would* care to see that scrapbook, and the photos too, the midget got up, and the two of them got on the elevator with the bellboy and went up to the midget's room.

When the bellboy had left, the midget took off his shirt and sat on the floor in his undershirt. He opened his suitcase and went jerking through his clothes, looking for the book, while the boy sat on the chair and watched. In a little while the midget found the large, flat scrapbook. He jumped up on the bed and sat with his cowboy boots hanging over the side.

He showed Sam pictures of himself in *Samson and Delilah,* and in *Never Too Soon,* and in a movie with John Garfield and Fred Astaire. There were also pictures of the midget in a circus, riding elephants and sitting on top of tigers, standing beside tall men under tents, and sitting in the laps of several different fat women, who were all laughing.

When they had looked at all the pictures and all the clippings, the midget said that he was sleepy after a long plane ride from the West Coast and that Sam would have to go, so that he could get some rest.

Sam shook hands with the midget, and the midget gave him an autographed picture of himself. Then the boy left.

When Sam came back to the lobby, his father was waiting for him, smoking a cigar. Sam showed him the picture of the midget with a laughing woman, and his father became upset. He tore up the picture and went to the glassed-in office beside the front desk, and had a long talk with the hotel manager while the boy waited outside. In a while his father came out and the two of them went home, where the boy's mother was sick.

Late in the night, Sam could hear his father and mother talking about the midget with the cowboy boots on. He heard his father say that the hotel manager had refused to have the midget thrown out of the hotel. Then, a little later, he heard his mother crying.

POEMS WRITTEN AFTER LOOKING AT
TWO JAPANESE DRAWINGS

Elizabeth Spires

FAT MAN

Clearly, the man eats too much.
He holds a half-eaten plum, reaches unthinking
toward the empty bowl for another one.
His manners are bad. He embarrasses his guests
by unfastening his pants, scolds
the thin children who break into his orchard
and find nothing. He thinks of himself as wise,
but look, he ignores the hovering butterfly,
smiles not at his wife, now approaching,
but at the fruit she carries.
More fruit for him.

GIRL MONKEY TRAINER

Her family was poor. Her feet big as brooms.
No one in the village would marry her.
One night she ran away, taking
the small amount that was to be her dowry.
She met a man on the road, a man
with two monkeys. He gave her one
for spending the night with him.
Now she lives far from the provinces, smiling
often at her good fortune. Her monkey performs
   well.
She buys herself silk scarves, has tea
whenever she wants it, rice cakes, wine.

LEAVIMA
✑ Don Belton

My mother name me Peanut she say because I was born so tiny for all the world and looking so full of possibilities. When she see how I growed up to love to run the streets, she use to tell me, "Daughter, there aint nothing in them streets." She was right. Aint nothing in the streets. I'm just learning that very thing, old as I am and still running them.

I wasn't a damn bit of good. I went straight on to Daddy Poole soon as I got into the bar life. All you could hear if you was a girl growing up in the life in Newark back then was Poole, his Cadillacs, and his women. When I come out into the street world, it was a day of mens—not like it is today. Black mens was pulling elevators and sweeping floors, working ice trucks and coal trucks, tearing apart automobiles for scrapyards—work what develop the muscles in shoulders and thighs. Or they might be cooks, dishwashers, or porters. They was shining shoes at the Pennsylvania Station. Plenty of them was preachers, and still they was hustling—selling produce, barbering, selling brushes for the Fuller Company. There was hit men and enforcers. The process-hair, sharp-dressing daddies was running their whores and running games, but most of them cool papas aint have no more going for them than what they had between their legs. Seem to me back then Daddy was more than a thousand mens.

Sure, he was handsome. He looked like old pictures of Duke Ellington and Cab Calloway, and nobody had the clothes Daddy use to wear. But to me the most sexy thing about him was his voice. You could hear him preaching over the radio on Sunday nights. He had that radio broadcast from his church over on Broome Street. And he use to be at Mr. Wonderful's when it was an all-night rhythm and blues bar. That was where the real rough hellbound soldiers too evil to ever enter a church might get to see him. He owned Mr. Wonderful's, so he was eating the colored district alive—having us both ways. He was getting rich off them house-rocking holy folks down on Broome Street, and he preach them so good down there they aint know or care he had a whole other money machine off of the Devil's children.

To give him his due, though, that's because he aint preach no Devil. Daddy preached everything was good. Everything was God. Then, too, I guess, there was plenty black people, along the time Poole come on the scene, was willing to see what would happen if you put the Devil on the same altar with Christ. Seem like aint nothing happen but prosperity. That's what Poole was, what his church was: the Devil on the same altar with Christ.

He'd be sitting back in the back room of Mr. Wonderful's like a king. You couldn't hardly see him for all the women what was around him. It was always smoky there, and sometimes I'd be looking in there all night and maybe not see no more of him than a diamond-flashing finger or his mustard-colored hand smoothing down the back of his hair. I was wearing so much makeup I musta looked like a freak. I knew I aint had what a lot of them other women had—nice breasts and a big behind—but I was determined to be one of Daddy Poole's women just the same. I was just a skinny kid with—in them days—long hair and a cute face. I had big eyes.

There was a singer was singing at Mr. Wonderful's named Leavima Hall—hollerer I should say instead of singer, but she had what it took to please the crowd what came to that place, and you had to be loud to get over all the noise always going on in there—sometimes fighting and cutting. Daddy was sweet on Leavima. She was his main queen at the time. So I went to work on her. I'd hang out in there till closing time, then I'd go up to the stand and tell her how much I liked her singing and shaking.

I guess she thought I was all right, because sometime when Daddy wasn't going to spend the night with her, Leavima would let me ride over to her apartment in the Cadillac with red bomber taillights Daddy gave her. She'd cook pepper steaks for us with mustard greens. I might press her clothes and straighten up her closets—I loved to look at all her nice things—or I might wash out her stockings. Leavima always kept plenty of reefer, and she showed me how to smoke it, but I aint like it because it just made me silly. She sang the rocking stuff for the people at Mr. Wonderful's, but Leavima could sing the hell out of just about everything. She used to sing real nice blues to me over at her apartment sometime, real light and sassy stuff. She'd be rocking back and forth like she was doing it with a fine, easy lover, her eyes would be closed: "My daddy rocks me, rocks me with a steady roll, every time he rock me, he sa-tis-fies my soul." She could make them blues sound almost like spirituals.

After a while Leavima started to pay me to be her personal maid. It wasn't long before I got to be there in the apartment when Daddy come around. He aint liked Leavima smoking as much reefer as she did, and that's what they would fight about. All the drugs he helped bring in Newark, and couldn't stand for her to smoke a damn reefer. She'd try to hide it, but you could smell it no matter what she do, the smell be all in her clothes and hair. Regardless how much Daddy would be on her for getting high, Leavima would stay tore up just the same. I believe her getting high was just her way of dealing with not having no real life. She sang and did her hip-working moves at the nightclub seven days a week. She'd come back to her crib and wait for him. She aint never go nowhere much. Daddy aint allow her to have no friends. She had me put on the payroll, but the biggest thing I was doing was keeping that girl company.

While she was on the set at Mr. Wonderful's, she always look like she was having a gas, singing and rattling her long earrings, but that shit aint mean nothing because couldn't nobody touch her up there on that stage. At home she stayed nervous most the time, and by me being around a lot I got to see how much she drank.

I ain't mind drinking with her. We liked Johnnie Walker Red. Leavima was good-looking, but I knew she was pimp crazy. You can tell when a woman been hurt by a whole lot of no-good pimps. She seemed together, but you could tell there was something inside her was ripping hell out of her. We ain't talk that much. It probably wasn't no big thing, no more than what's the matter with a lot of women—feeling like whatever they is and what life give them aint never going to be enough, like they missed the train. And can't never catch up. But when she was on the set she was laid and happening, till one night she had a seizure in the middle of singing a Ruth Brown song.

When Daddy brung her back from the hospital he got it out of her she'd been taking over a gram of cocaine a day, and the cocaine had caused her seizure. She'd been blowing that much coke out the fat allowance Daddy give her and trying to clean up her shit by telling him she taking the blow because her nerves is bad.

"Bitch," Daddy told her, "your ass is going to be bad if you don't straighten up."

He actually loved that girl. He'd been going with Leavima for damn near a year, and he still hadn't turned her out to prostitution. But she just wasn't all there mentally. You had to really be around her to see it. Daddy warned her how he was going to do her if she aint straighten herself up. She aint listen. He couldn't take the shit from her no faster than she would get some more stashed someplace. They say you graduate from one drug to another, and in Leavima case it was a true saying. When Daddy caught her skin-popping the Big Boy— heroin—he finally gave up on her and cut her loose. He aint have no more use for her then.

He closed her out at Mr. Wonderful's and brung in a jazzy combo. He had Leavima took down to a building by the docks—down in the Neck. All her clothes was took away from her—her car, her jewelry, everything. She was locked in a bathroom down there, and men paid to go in the bathroom and have her. How long Daddy had her doing bathroom tricks or what happen to her after that I don't know and didn't care, because when he got rid of her, it was me he put in her place. That was the beginning of me being a whore for Daddy Poole.

MOODY
⋖ Alice Walker

I am a moody woman
my temper as black as my brows
as sharp as my nails
as impartial as a flood
that is seeking, seeking, seeking
always
somewhere to stop.

MORNING LIGHT
Linda Pastan

How many times do we try
to start our lives
all over again?
Every morning, perhaps,
rising out of the ruins
of sleep, putting the things
of the night away
as if we are stowing
our gear on a ship
about to take off for someplace new,
someplace distant.
There is something about the slant
of the morning light,
the way it pushes its gilded prow
into the leftover air
so that the dust motes tremble
and open into a path
we can follow.
For a moment, charged
with coffee, it seems

possible to do anything,
if only we knew
what it was
that was wanted.

THE WAY I FEEL
Nikki Giovanni

i've noticed i'm happier
when i make love
with you
and have enough left
over to smile at my doorman

i've realized i'm fulfilled
like a big fat cow
who was just picked
for a carnation contentment
when you kiss your special place
right behind my knee

i'm glad as mortar
on a brick that knows
another brick is coming
when you walk through
my door

most time when you're around
i feel like a note
roberta flack is going to sing

in my mind you're a clock
and i'm the second hand sweeping
around you sixty times an hour
twenty-four hours a day
three hundred sixty-five days a year
and an extra day
in leap year
'cause that's the way
that's the way
that's the way I feel
about you

AUTUMN POEMS

Nikki Giovanni

the heat
you left with me
last night
still smolders
the wind catches
your scent
and refreshes
my senses

i am a leaf
falling from your tree
upon which i was
impaled

AT SIXTY
◁§ Dennis Brutus

Even at sixty
as sap leaps with the spring,
lust flames in my blood.

AT THE MEMORIAL WALL

Adapted by Bobbie Ann Mason from her novel
In Country

When Samantha Hughes (Sam in this story) is born, her father is dead, killed in Vietnam. By the time Sam is eighteen, her mother has remarried and has moved out of Kentucky, to another state.

Sam now lives with her uncle Emmett, a troubled Vietnam veteran, who Sam thinks is suffering from exposure to Agent Orange, the poison sprayed over the forests of Vietnam to destroy them.

Mamaw Hughes is Sam's grandmother—the mother of Sam's dead father, Dwayne Hughes.

In this story, the last chapter of the novel *In Country,* Sam Hughes, her uncle Emmett Smith, and Mamaw Hughes drive from Kentucky to Washington, D.C., to see the great black stone wall that is the national Vietnam Veterans Memorial.

They have come to find the name Dwayne E. Hughes that is carved in the wall alongside the names of the 58,000 other Americans who died in Vietnam.

As they drive into Washington, Sam feels unsettled, almost sick. She keeps telling herself that the memorial is only a rock with names on it. It doesn't mean anything except they're dead. It's just names. Nobody here but us chickens. Just us and the planet Earth and the nuclear bomb. But that's okay, she thinks now. Nobody here but us.

Maybe that's the point. People shouldn't make too much of death. Her history teacher said there are more people alive now than dead. He warned that there were so many people alive now, and they were living so much longer, that people had the idea they were just about immortal. But everyone's going to die, and we'd better get used to the idea, he said. Dead and gone. Long gone from Kentucky.

Sometimes in the middle of the night it struck Sam that she was going to die someday. Most of the time she forgot about this. But now, as she and Emmett and Mamaw Hughes drive into Washington to the Vietnam Memorial where the names of so many who died are cut into the stone, the fact of death hits her in broad daylight. Mamaw is fifty-eight. She could die soon. She could die any minute, like that racehorse that keeled over dead for no reason on Father's Day. Also Sam has been afraid Emmett would die from Agent Orange. But Emmett came looking for her that night she got lost in the swamp, because it was unbearable to him that *she* might die.

The Washington Monument is a gleaming pencil against the sky. Emmett is driving, and the traffic is

BOOK THREE *Words on the Page,*

frightening. They pass cars with government license plates that say FED. Sam wonders how long the Washington Monument will stand on the earth.

A sign on Constitution Avenue says VIETNAM VETERANS MEMORIAL. Emmett can't find a parking place nearby. He parks on a side street, and they walk toward the Washington Monument. Mamaw puffs along. She has put on a good dress and stockings. Sam feels they are walking too slowly. She wants to break into a run. The Washington Monument rises up out of the earth, proud and tall. The buildings they pass are so pretty, so white. In Sam's dream, the Vietnam Memorial was a black boomerang, whizzing toward her head.

"I don't see it," Mamaw says.

"It's over yonder," Emmett says, pointing. "They say you come up on it sudden."

"My legs are starting to hurt."

Sam wants to run, but she doesn't know whether she wants to run toward the memorial or away from it. She just wants to run. Emmett is carrying a pot of geraniums. Sam feels his secret suffering. His heart must be racing, as if something unbearable is about to happen.

Emmett holds Mamaw's arm and carefully steers her across the street. The pot of geraniums hugs his chest.

"There it is," Sam says. It is enormous, a black gash in a hillside, like a vein of coal exposed and then polished to a high shine. A crowd is filing by slowly, staring at it solemnly.

"Law," says Sam's grandmother quietly. "It's black as night."

"Here's the directory," Emmett says, as they come to the entrance. "I'll look up his name for you, Mrs. Hughes."

Sam stands in the shade, looking at the black wing sunk so deep in the soil that there is grass growing above it. It is like a giant grave with fifty-eight thousand bodies rotting here behind the names. The people are streaming past, down into the pit.

"It don't show up good," Mamaw says. "It's just a hole in the ground."

The memorial cuts a V in the ground, like the wings of a bird, huge and headless. Overhead, a jet plane angles upward, taking off.

"He's on Panel 9E," Emmett reports. "That's on the east wing. We're on the west."

Flowers are placed here and there against the bottom of the wall. A little kid says, "Look, Daddy, the flowers are dying." The man snaps back, "Some are and some aren't."

A woman in a sun hat points a camera at the wall. She says to the woman with her, "I didn't think it would look like this. Things aren't what you think they look like. I didn't know it was a wall."

A stiff-legged guy in old army clothing walks by with a cane. Probably he has an artificial leg, Sam thinks, but he walks along proudly, as if he has been there many times before and doesn't have any particular business at the moment. He seems to belong here.

A group of schoolkids tumbles through, noisy as chickens. One of the girls says, "Are they piled up on top of each other?" They walk on a few steps and she says, "What are all these names anyway?"

Sam feels like punching the girl in the face for being so dumb. How could anybody that age not know? But she realizes that she doesn't know, either. She is just beginning to understand. And she will never really know what happened to all these men in the war. Some people walk by, talking as though they are on a Sunday picnic, but most are reverent, and some of them are crying.

Sam stands in the center of the V, deep in the pit. The V is like the two wings of the shopping mall back home. The Washington Monument is reflected at the center line. If she moves a little to the left, she sees the monument, and if she moves the other way, she sees the reflection of a flag. Both the monument and the flag seem like ugly gestures, like the country giving the finger to the dead boys, piled up in this hole in the ground.

Sam doesn't understand what she is feeling, but it is something strong. It is like a tornado moving in her, something huge and overpowering. It feels like giving birth to this wall.

"I wish Tom could be here," Sam says to Emmett. "He needs to be here." Her voice is thin like smoke, and hard to hear.

"He'll make it here someday. Jim's coming too. They're all coming one of these days."

"Are you going to look for anybody's name besides my daddy's?"

"Yeah."

"Who?"

"Those guys I told you about, the ones that died all around me. And a guy I was going to look up here in D.C.—he might be on the wall. I don't know if he made it out or not."

Sam gets a flash of Emmett's suffering. He has been grieving for fourteen years. A jet plane flies overhead, close to the earth. Its wings are angled back too, like a bird's.

Two workmen in hard hats are there with a stepladder and some loud machinery. One of the workmen, whose hat says on the back NEVER AGAIN, seems to be drilling in the wall.

"What's he doing, hon?" Sam hears Mamaw say behind her.

"It looks like they're patching up a hole or something."

The man on the ladder turns off the tool, a sander, and the other workman hands him a brush. He brushes the spot. The name he is working on is highlighted in yellow, as though someone had taken a Magic Marker and colored it, the way Sam used to mark names and dates, important facts, in her schoolbooks.

"Somebody must have vandalized it," says a man behind Sam. "Can you imagine the sicko who would do that?"

"No," says the woman with him. "Somebody just wanted the name to stand out and be noticed. I can go with that."

Sam gazes at the flowers placed along the base of the memorial. A white carnation is stuck in a crack between two panels of the wall. A woman bends down and smooths a ribbon on a wreath. The ribbon has gold letters on it, "VFW Post 7215."

They are moving slowly. Panel 9E is some distance ahead. Sam reads a small poster propped at the base of the wall: "To those men of C Company, 173rd Airborne, who were lost in the battle for Hill 823, Nov. 11, 1967. Because of their bravery I am here today. A grateful buddy."

A man rolls by in a wheelchair. Another jet plane flies over.

A handwritten note taped to the wall apologizes to one of the names for leaving him behind in a firefight.

Mamaw turns to fuss over the geraniums in Emmett's arms, the way she might fluff a pillow.

Sam watches two uniformed marines searching and searching for a name. "He must be along here somewhere," one says. They keep looking, running their hands over the names.

"There it is. That's him."

They read his name and both look quickly away, stare out for a moment in the direction of the Lincoln Memorial, then walk briskly off.

"May I help you find someone's name?" asks a woman with a clipboard in her hand. She is a park guide.

"We know where we are," Emmett says. "Much obliged, though."

At panel 9E, Sam stands back while Emmett and Mamaw search for her father's name.

"There it is," Emmett says. The name is above his head, near the top of the wall. He reaches up and touches it. "There's his name, Dwayne E. Hughes."

"I can't reach it," says Mamaw. "Oh, I wanted to touch it," she says softly.

"We'll set the flowers here, Mrs. Hughes," says Emmett. He sets the pot at the base of the panel, tenderly, as though he is tucking in a baby.

"I'm going to bawl," Mamaw says, bowing her head and starting to sob. "I wish I could touch it."

Sam has an idea. She runs over to the workmen and asks them to let her borrow the stepladder. One of them brings it over and sets it up beside the wall. Sam urges Mamaw to climb the ladder, but Mamaw holds back. "No. I can't do it. You do it."

"Go ahead, ma'am," the workman says.

"Emmett and me'll hold the ladder," says Sam.

"Somebody might see up my dress."

"No, go on, Mrs. Hughes. You can do it," says Emmett. "Come on, we'll help you reach it."

He takes her arm. Together, he and Sam steady her while she places her foot on the first step and swings herself up. She seems scared, and she doesn't speak. She reaches up but cannot touch the name.

"One more, Mamaw," says Sam, looking up at her grandmother—at the sagging wrinkles, her flab hanging loose and sad, and her eyes red with crying. Mamaw reaches toward the name and struggles up the next step, holding her dress tight against her. She touches the name, running her hand over it, stroking it carefully, affectionately. Her chin wobbles, and after a moment she backs down the ladder silently.

When Mamaw is down, Sam starts up the ladder.

"Here, take the camera, Sam. Get his name." Mamaw has brought the Instamatic.

"No, I can't take a picture this close."

Sam climbs the ladder until she is eye level with her father's name. She feels funny touching it.

"Look this way, Sam," Mamaw says. "I want to take your picture. I want to get you and his name and the flowers in together if I can."

"The name won't show up," Sam says.

"Smile."

"How can I smile?" She is crying.

Mamaw backs up and snaps two pictures. From up on the ladder Sam sees Emmett at the directory, probably searching for his buddies' names. She touches her father's name again.

"All I can see from here is my reflection," Mamaw

says when Sam comes down the ladder. "I hope his name shows up. And your face was all shadow."

"Wait here a minute," Sam says, turning away her tears from Mamaw.

She runs to the directory, but Emmett isn't there anymore. She sees him striding along the wall, searching for a name.

Sam flips through the directory and finds "Hughes." She wants to see her father's name here too. She runs her finger down the row of Hughes names. There were so many Hughes boys killed, names she doesn't know. Her father's name is there, and she gazes at it for a moment. Then suddenly her own name leaps out at her.

SAM ALAN HUGHES

14E 104

Her heart is pounding. She rushes to panel 14E, and after racing her eyes over the string of names, she locates her own name.

SAM A HUGHES. It is on a first line. It is down low enough to touch. She touches her own name. How odd it feels, as though all the names in America have been written on this wall.

Mamaw is at her side, pulling at Sam's arm, digging in with her fingernails. Mamaw says, "Coming up on this wall of a sudden and seeing how black it was, it was so awful. But then I came down in it and saw that white carnation blooming out of the crack, and it gave me hope. It made me know he's watching over us." She loosens her bird-claw grip. "Did we lose Emmett?"

Silently, Sam points to the place where Emmett is studying the names on a low panel. He is sitting cross-legged in front of the wall, and slowly his face bursts into a smile like flames.

VIETNAM MEMORIAL
❦ Karl Shapiro

It lies on its side in the grassy Mall,
A capsized V, a skeletal
Half-sunken hull of a lost cause
Between the Washington Monument and the
   Capitol.

To see it you descend a downward path
And stare up at the blackened decks of names,
Army of names that holds this empty tomb
Shimmering in shadow in the flashing gloom.

Topside you can hear children at their games,
Down in this trench there is no gab.
Someone lay flowers under a name that was,
Our eyes like seaworms crawl across this slab.

Coasting the fifty thousand here who died.
We surface breathless, come up bleary-eyed.

WHEN THEY TOOK HIM AWAY
Frank M. Chipasula

They did not give him time
to kiss his children or stroke
his wife before leaving.
My brother did not weep.

They bundled him roughly
into the Black Maria, chained,
guarded, drove him to the grill.
My brother did not weep.

They emptied his soul
on the counter and dressed him
in DT's uniform without collars.
My brother only smiled.

They shoved him into the torture
chamber like wood into a furnace
and scorched him with their scourges.
My brother did not cry.

He smiled as they chained him
hand to leg, sliced his back with
hippo hide welts, drawing blood.

In the punishment cell
they placed ice blocks all over him;
they stung and sucked his blood.
My brother did not groan.

He smiled as he wilted into a leaf
they thought they could grind on the
hard concrete floor in the solitary cell.
My brother did not flinch.

After a year, only twice visited,
without a book for dialogue, without a voice,
without an ear, he staggered out tall

He did not fall.
He kept on smiling.

CATENA
(COMMEMORATING THE VICTIMS OF SOWETO)
∾ *Dennis Brutus*

Pray you, remember them.

The alleys reeking with the acrid stench
of gunfire, tear gas, and arrogant hate

Pray you, remember them
                         (We remember them)

The pungent odor of anger,
of death and dying, and decay

I pray you, do remember them
                         (We remember them)

Anger drifting through smoke-filled lanes
in sudden erratic gusts

Pray and remember
                         (We remember them)

Torn bodies half glimpsed
Through standing roiling smoke

Pray, remember them
                    (We remember them)

The Ghettos reeking
Fathers grieving
Mothers weeping
Bodies of children torn and bleeding

Pray, remember them: We remember them.

CLAUDIO'S VISION
◆§ Robert Coles

I met Claudio in Florida fifteen years ago. I was
talking with the children of migrant farm workers, who
lived in a town called Immokalee. Many of these children were black, many were of Mexican ancestry but
had become American citizens. They were known as
Mexican-Americans, though some of them called themselves Chicanos. Earlier in this century white families
had harvested Florida's crops, but by the time I became
interested in the lives of migrant children in that state,
black and Spanish-speaking families were the only ones
I ever saw in the many "camps" for migrant families.

Among the boys and girls I met in Immokalee, one
lad of ten has stood out in my memory. He was quite a
hardworking boy, known by everyone in Immokalee as
the fastest picker around of beans and peas and
tomatoes. He came to work early in the morning and left
only when darkness arrived. He worked from sunup to
sundown. His friends would ask him why he wanted to
work such long hours, and he always replied with the
same three words: "To make money." But then the
friends wanted to know what he intended to do with the
money—because he was also known as a picky eater, a

ragged dresser, and "a stingy stroller," meaning that when he and his friends took their walks, he was rarely interested in buying candy or a toy. Claudio did tell everyone that he loved ice cream; but he was rarely seen eating it. Once he bought five ice pops for his five pals, as they took an evening stroll—yet he refused to get one for himself. He claimed a sick stomach.

Claudio was an orphan. His mother had died giving birth to him. An enormous blood clot, lodged in a vein somewhere below her waistline, had moved up suddenly to her lungs and killed her. His father had been killed in an accident: he and several other farm workers had been crushed by a truck that veered into the bus that was taking them to work early one May morning. Claudio had become, at three, his aunt's son. Claudio's aunt was also a hardworking farm worker, the mother of six children besides Claudio, her adopted son.

Despite the hard work Claudio did, and the hard life he and others he knew lived, he was a cheerful ten-year-old and was always willing to take the time to sit and talk with me about his life, his hopes and worries, and, not least, his future. One day, we talked about what he envisioned for himself ten years or so down the road, when he'd be a young man of twenty. He stopped the discussion in its tracks and reminded me that no one could say for sure whether he or she would be around tomorrow, never mind years and years ahead.

Most children, I have learned, don't think of life as something that can suddenly be ended by a stroke of bad luck. But Claudio, as an orphan, had good reason. Children don't often speak of death, at least not of their own death. They *assume* life, and they announce what they will do with it. Claudio was more guarded, as he let me know in this way:

"I could be called at any moment," he said. "If I got the call, I'd say yes, I knew I might be called. I'd try to smile and not be upset. I wouldn't want to leave my friends, because I know lots of people, but I'd go without a fight. That's the way to go."

He stopped abruptly at that point and had nothing more to say. I was puzzled by his words. I wanted to ask him who might be the one to "call" him. I wanted to ask him how he had come to take such a view of death—as a summons by someone. But his face, then, did not invite such questions from me. He was looking at his left hand, and picking at a wart on the end of its finger.

Suddenly he changed the subject. He told me that he had several warts on his hand and said they were a nuisance. He showed them to me. Then he pointed out that his body had other troubles. He had bruises on his knees—all the kneeling to do all the harvesting. He had cuts and bruises on his hands as well, for the same reason. As he looked at the costs of his work, the scars of his life's daily battles, he returned to his warts and contemplated them: "The public health nurse said they are 'growths.' I like them! They prove that my body can grow! I like the bumps on my hands too. The tougher my hands, the better they are for picking!

"I had a dream last night. I was picking beans. My knees hurt. My hands hurt. I had a bad headache from the sun. I was very thirsty, but there was no water to drink. I wanted to keep picking, but my hands were not doing what they were supposed to. My legs weren't working. They seemed stuck in the muck. I looked up at the sky. The sun stared me down. I looked at a cloud, moving slowly across the sky.

"I saw a face; it was the picture of my mother that my father had kept for me. It's what he left me. I keep it with my rosary beads. In my dream, my mother's picture was pinned to the cloud. I wanted it back here. I stood up to reach for it. Somehow, I got it back. Maybe it fell from the sky! I put it in my pocket, and then I felt stronger. My legs moved; so did my hands. I got through the row of beans. The owner was there, and he paid me, and he gave me an extra dollar. I put all the money in the same place."

When he'd finished telling me his dream, I was silent. He didn't seem as sad as I felt. I decided I had to say something, to ask something, to show my interest in what he had told me. He did not deserve pity from me; and clearly he wanted no consolation. He was proud that even in his dream he finished the job he had set out to do. Suddenly I remembered that he had mentioned a "place" where he had put his earnings. He had put his small bonus "in the same place." I became curious, and I spoke: "What place is it where you put your money?" He lowered his head and said nothing. A few seconds passed. I tried to find a new question, or a comment to break the silence. I felt that I had violated the boy's privacy—his sense that where he put his cash earnings was no one's business but his. I said something about the intense heat of the day; and the boy shrugged it off: "Yes, but it is hot here all the time now." We continued with weather talk for a while, and then he had to go.

A month later, a priest talked with me about the children who did the long, tough daily job of harvesting crops. He interrupted his description to tell me a story about one special child:

"He is one of our best workers. He is like lightning—the way he works his way up and down the rows of vegetables. No one knows something about him that I do. He brings his money to me. He brings a picture of his mother to me also. He insists that I take the money and bless his mother's picture. He wants me to use the money to buy food and clothes for others here! There are so many who have so little! He gives me half of what he earns. He is so fast that he still has enough to get by with the half he keeps for himself and gives to his aunt. He always says a prayer before and after giving me the money. He concentrates on that picture of his mother. He sees her, I guess, in his mind. Sometimes he pictures himself meeting her in heaven. A child's vision!"

Then he paused, and I decided to tell him that I thought I knew who the boy was. I mentioned my friendship with Claudio and the conversations we'd had over the months. "Yes," the priest said, "you are right; it is

Claudio." We were both at a loss for words—until the priest added this thought: "When that boy comes here, so generous and kind, I have my own vision. He thinks of his mother, and I think of God. I feel the good Lord visits us here through Claudio."

When he had spoken those words, I felt no need to say anything, nor apparently did he. After a few seconds I noticed that my head, for some reason, was bent; and when I looked at the priest, I noticed that his head, too, was bent.

WHAT HAS HAPPENED
TO THESE WORKING HANDS?

Linda Hogan

They opened the ground and closed it around seeds.
They added a pinch of tobacco.
They cleaned tired old bodies
    and bathed infants.
They got splinters from the dried-out handles of axes.
The right one suspected what the left was doing
    and the arms began to ache.
They clawed at each other when life hurt.
They pulled at my hair when I mourned.
They tangled my hair when I dreamed poems.
As fists they hit the bed when war spread through the
        papers.
They went crazy and broke glasses.
They regretted going to school because they became so soft
    their relatives mistook them for strangers.
They turned lamps off and on
    and tapped out songs on tables,
        made crosses over the heart.
They kneaded bread.
They covered my face when I cried,
    my mouth when I laughed.

"You've got troubles," said the left hand to the right.
 "Here, let me hold you."
These hands untwisted roots buried too long.
They drummed the old burial songs.
They heard there were men cruel enough to crush them.
They drummed the old buried songs.

AN OBSERVATION

May Sarton

True gardeners cannot bear a glove
Between the sure touch and the tender root,
Must let their hands grow knotted as they move
With a rough sensitivity about
Under the earth, between the rock and shoot,
Never to bruise or wound the hidden fruit.
And so I watched my mother's hands grow scarred,
She who could heal the wounded plant or friend
With the same vulnerable yet rigorous love;
I minded once to see her beauty gnarled,
But now her truth is given me to live,
As I learn for myself we must be hard
To move among the tender with an open hand,
And to stay sensitive up to the end,
Pay with some toughness for a gentle world.

TWO FOALS

Adapted by Maxine Kumin from her book In Deep

I am writing in my journal in the blackness of the barn while waiting for a baby horse to be born. This page is lit by a troublelight, the kind that auto workers use. It hangs from a nail over my head.

In horse talk, the mother horse is called a mare. The baby will be called a foal. This spring, five horses live here in box stalls. Two of them are pregnant mares, and they live in the biggest stalls.

Sawdust bedding is heaped in a bin next to the last stall. This week I am sleeping in the bin on the flat top of the heap. Under me are two foam pads. Although it is the middle of May, the nights are cool and damp, and I wear long johns inside my old sleeping bag.

It's a cozy bed, even though the old cotton batting smells musty. Abra and Cadabra, sister barn cats, sleep on my feet. I can check on the mare from time to time by raising up on one elbow to peer over the stall side. Although her milkbag is full and hard, night after night she holds back from having her baby. In horse talk, we call this dropping her foal.

I see this as a tug-of-war. She wants to have her foal in private. I, on the other hand, want to be there. This

mare lost her first foal a few years ago. No one was able to find out why it did not breathe when it was born. I blamed myself then. That blame is with me still.

This time I mean to stand by to break the sac the foal is born in. I will do mouth-to-mouth breathing; I will even pull on a plastic sleeve and reach in to free a stuck shoulder. I have never done any of these things. I am not sure I *can* do them. But I have gone to lectures, and I have studied drawings of wrong positions, where the foal comes out feet first or sideways. I hope I know enough to do the right thing.

In the meantime, I overhear every rustle, munch, and snore. There is no getting away from my watchful eye. If the mare lies down, I wake up. When she lies down to sleep with one front leg pressing against her throat, her snoring is louder than rock-and-roll music. The whole barn shakes.

If the mare gets up from lying down, I wake up too. I'm there on one elbow with my flashlight to see if everything is still the same. In the sweet-smelling dark, our eyes meet. Hers are a burning wild red. I wonder what she thinks of mine, which do not glow at night.

But at dawn the world begins all over again. She is happy to have me on the spot. She puts her nose up over the top board and nickers in a soft way that sounds like the cooings of large doves. She would like to be fed, she says.

I groan getting up. I open the old chest freezer we keep feed in. I scoop out her two quarts of grain, sprinkle the top with the right vitamins for pregnant mares. Then, trailing my sleeping bag like a long tail, I make for my own bed across the road. I feel safe doing this because I know the mare will not go into labor in daylight.

The first mare's foal this spring came at two in the morning. She did not have it the way the book says, however. The horse books all say that a mare in labor will act uncomfortable. She will walk back and forth, get up, lie down, perhaps permit herself a few grunts. She will at least rustle around in her stall. Suzy, my horse helper, who was foal-watching that week and sleeping so lightly that the local hoot owl woke her every night, heard no warning noises. What woke her was the sound of rushing water. She saw that the sac had broken and buzzed Victor on the intercom.

By the time Victor had pulled on his jeans and run across the road to the barn, the little foal had swum out of the mare, nose first, the right way. It was a female foal. In horse talk, a female foal is called a filly. The mare and the filly lay quietly talking, exchanging little nuzzles and nickers. After ten minutes or so, the mare arose and licked her baby filly all over quite roughly. In another few minutes the little one was able to stand up and start nursing.

This is called bonding, and bonding is just an instinct. Wise men tell us that instinct is just something we are born with. But I call it a miracle.

The day after the first foal slipped so easily into the world, the second pregnant mare comes in from her outdoor shed for the evening meal. She sniffs it but does not touch it. Since she is a very greedy eater, we know Her Time Has Come. I settle down quietly out of sight. At last I am going to watch a foal being born.

The mare, while not upset, is clearly restless. She lies down, gets up, lies down again. I can see the contractions move in waves down her sides. Her chest is wet with sweat. Calmly, I wait.

Daylight fades. The contractions stop. The mare gets up, shakes herself, walks over to her feedbox, and licks up every last grain of oats. She then begins on the fresh straw we have used to bed her stall thickly. A straw bed for giving birth is said to be safer for mother and foal than sawdust. It is also very expensive, at least in New England—about twice the price of good hay.

I sleep very well that night on the sawdust heap. I have one ear tuned to the engine of her digestion running as the mare chews her way through all the bedding.

The next evening the mare tucks into her grain at once, then dives into her pile of hay. Mares are supposed to go off their feed before foaling, so I am feeling a little grim about my long life on the sawdust heap. But wait! Something has happened. Two little drops of wax have formed on her teats. Everyone agrees on the meaning of this wax. It is a special milk called colostrum. Once this colostrum appears, the mare will drop her foal in a few hours. Although she is simply hanging out looking relaxed and full, Suzy and I agree to take turns checking the mare every ten minutes.

After making several trips to the barn, we agree that nothing will happen before 8 or 9 P.M. The mare will wait for what is called in mystery stories "the cover of darkness."

Suzy goes off to wash her hair. I make another trip across the road to the barn. No change. Suzy dries her hair. I toss the salad. We are ready to sit down to supper. Suzy trots down to the barn once more.

I hear her yelling before I see her racing back to the house. In eight minutes, the mare has foaled, and mother and baby are both on their feet.

So much for "cover of darkness." So much for my sharp eye, sawdust nights, plastic sleeves. What we find is a wet, wobbly baby. It bops from corner to corner, bumping into walls, feed tub, water bucket. For one long minute I think something terrible is wrong with it. We catch it and look underneath to see what we have—another filly! We paint the navel stump with iodine. More than an hour passes before the little one is calm enough and hungry enough to find her way to the mare's big milkbag.

The poor mare goes from nickers of welcome to squeals of pain as that hungry mouth fastens onto her teats. Gradually, though, the foal's sucking relieves their fullness, and with it the pain. Suzy spends one more night on the sawdust pile to be sure the two are firmly bonded.

Now we have a second miracle. This one is fawn-colored, turning toward red, with a white streak running down her face in the shape of South America.

What luck to have two fillies! On the family farm, a male foal is called a colt. He has to be cut or gelded while he is still young. Otherwise he will try to breed the mares. A filly, when she grows up, can be bred to carry on the bloodline. I dream of fields of playful foals, better and better mares to come.

The first week of fillies is one of great caution. We have two very protective mares, two friendly foals. The later-born filly does not seem to know one brown mother's rump from the other and sometimes asks the wrong mother to let her suck. Neither mare will let her baby have anything to do with the other one.

A certain amount of rushing around with ears back takes place. There are some strong trumpet calls to bring the wandering babies back to their mothers' sides. And I had forgotten how shrill the calls of foals can be and how sadly they nicker when they get lost for a moment.

Our pastures are so hilly that we have set aside our one almost flat field especially for this first month out in the world. There is a shady stand of pines at one end. The rest is wall-to-wall grass and clover. Getting to it, though, means we have to climb a steep hill dotted with water bars. Putting halters on and leading two skittish foals up this hill is a daily trek into the mountains, led by our wise old spotted dog, whom the mares trust.

Although they were born only two days apart, the fillies are very different. One is big, chesty, and sure of herself, with a wonderful long stride. The other is fine, slender, spooky, and as fast as greased lightning. Now that they are turned out on these two acres, I can see why it was such a good idea to save this field for them. Once they start running, it looks as though the foals can never stop short of the fence boards. Somehow they always do, but I watch with my heart jumping into my mouth.

Now, at the end of June, the mothers have taken up their old friendship. They graze side by side, often standing head to rump to take advantage of each other's fanning tail. The six-week-old babies lie down a lot, often out of sight behind the screen of daisies and Indian paintbrush. At some magical moment two weeks ago, a law was passed by the mares that said the little ones could play with each other.

Now, unless thirsty or frightened, they ignore their mothers and stay together. One is the hub of the wheel; the other races in circles around her. They touch noses, whinny, spin, and leap. They crop grass together as best they can with their short necks, straining to reach the green stuff between their widely spread front legs. Perhaps a bird startles them, or the wind makes a tree branch creak, and they are off again, doing spins and twirls.

I spend a lot of time hanging over the fence this summer. The ballet goes on and on, in living color, and I never tire of it.

The hay is not in, the garden barely planted. Half of next winter's wood is still to be split and stacked. But this is the year of two fillies, two births with happy outcomes.

Even though I didn't get to see either one of the fillies being born, it is a magical summer. A summer of dancing foals and fat brown nursing mares with their noses in sweet green grass. A summer of happiness.

CELEBRATION: BIRTH OF A COLT

◄§ *Linda Hogan*

When we reach the field
she is still eating
the heads of yellow flowers
and pollen has turned her whiskers
gold. Lady,
her stomach bulges out,
the ribs have grown wide.
We wait,
our bare feet dangling
in the horse trough,
warm water
where the goldfish brush
our smooth ankles.
We wait
while the liquid breaks
down Lady's dark legs
and that slick wet colt
like a black tadpole
darts out
beginning at once
to sprout legs.
She licks it to its feet,

the membrane still there,
red,
transparent
the sun coming up shines through.
The sky turns bright with morning
and the land,
with pollen blowing off the corn,
land that will always own us,
everywhere is red.

WINTER SCENE
◄§ A. R. Ammons

There is now not a single
leaf on the cherry tree:

except when the jay
plummets in, lights, and,

in pure clarity, squalls:
then every branch

quivers and
breaks out in blue leaves.

EVOLUTION

◄§ May Swenson

The stone would like to be alive like me.
The rooted tree longs to be free.
The mute beast envies my fate, articulate.
On this ball, half dark, half light, I walk upright.
I lie prone within the night.
Beautiful each shape to see.
Wonderful each thing to name.
Here a stone, there a tree.
Here a river, there a flame.
Marvelous to stroke the patient beasts within their
   yoke.
How I yearn for the lion in his den
Though he spurn the touch of men.
The longing that I know is in the stone also.
It must be the same that rises in the tree.
The longing in the lion's call speaks for all.
Oh, to endure like the stone, sufficient to itself
   alone.
Or, reincarnate like the tree, be born each spring
   to greenery.
Or, like the lion without law, to roam the wind on
   velvet paw.

But if walking I meet a creature like me on the
   street,
Two-legged, with human face, to recognize is to
   embrace.
Wonders pale, beauties dim during my delight with
   him.
An evolution strange, two tongues touch, exchange
A feast unknown to stone or tree or beast.

THREE WAYS OF A RIVER
◀§ David Wagoner

Sometimes, without a murmur, the river chooses
　　The clearest channels, the easy ways
Downstream, dividing at islands equally, smoothly,
And meeting itself once more on the far side
　　In a gathering of seamless eddies
That blend so well, no ripples rise to break

Into light like fingerlings taking their first mayflies
　　Or, again, it will rush at overhangs
And blunder constantly against bare stone,
Against some huge implacable rock face
　　To steepen and plunge, spring wide, go white,
And be dashed in tatters of spray, revolved and
　　　　scattered

Like rain clouds pouring forward against a cliff
　　In an endless storm of its own making,
While calmly a foot away lies the shape all
　　water
Becomes if it flows aside into a pool,
　　As still as the rock that holds it, as level
As if held cold to drink in these two hands.

The World in Your Hands

THINGS
◁§ *Donald Justice*

STONE

Hard, but you can polish it.
Precious, it has eyes. Can wound.
Would dance upon water. Sinks.
Stays put. Crushed, becomes a road.

PILLOW

Mine to give, mine to offer
No resistance. Mine
To receive you, mine to keep
The shape of our nights.

MIRROR

My former friend, my traitor.
My too easily broken.
My still to be escaped from.

SALT

❧ Robert Francis

Salt for white
And salt for pure.
What's salted right
Will keep and cure.

Salt for cheap
And salt for free.
The poor may reap
Salt from the sea.

Salt for taste
And salt for wit.
Be wise. Don't waste
A pinch of it.

SEAWIND: A SONG

◆§ Donald Justice

Seawind, you rise
From the night waves below,
Not that we see you come and go,
But as the blind know things we know
And feel you on our face,
And all you are
Or ever were is space,

Seawind, come from so far,
To fill us with this restlessness
That will outlast your own—

So the fig tree,
When you are gone,
Seawind, still bends and leans out toward the sea
And goes on blossoming alone.

JOSEPH AND HIS BROTHERS

Adapted from the Bible story by Lore Segal

And Joseph was a young boy of seventeen and tended the sheep with his brothers, the sons of his father's wives, and Joseph came to their father, Jacob, and told tales on them.

Jacob loved Joseph best because he was the child of his old age, and he made him a coat of many colors. The brothers saw that their father loved Joseph best, and they hated him and never said a kind word to him.

And Joseph had a dream and told it to his brothers. He said, Listen to this dream that I have dreamed. We were binding sheaves of grain in the fields, and my sheaf stood up and remained standing, and your sheaves stood in a ring around my sheaf and bowed down before it.

His brothers said, You'd like to be a king, wouldn't you, and rule over us. And they hated him all the more, because of his dream.

And Joseph had another dream, and said, Come and hear another dream that I have dreamed. The sun, the moon, and eleven stars all bowed down before me.

He told his dream to his father, and his father became angry and said, What kind of a dream is that for you to be dreaming! Are we to come, your mother and I and all of your brothers, and bow ourselves down to the ground before you?

His brothers were jealous, but his father kept these things in his mind.

One day he said to Joseph, Come! Your brothers are grazing the flocks in the fields of Shechem. I want you to go and see how they are, and how the flocks are doing, and come back and tell me.

Joseph left and came to Shechem. And a certain man found him wandering in a field and asked him, What are you looking for?

He said, I'm looking for my brothers. Can you tell me where they have gone to graze their flocks?

The man said, I heard them talking. They said, Let's go on to Dothan.

Joseph followed his brothers to Dothan. They saw him coming from afar and made a plan how they might kill him. They said, Here comes the dreamer! Let's kill him and throw him in a pit in the ground. We'll say a wild animal devoured him; then we shall see what will become of all his dreams.

Reuben, the oldest brother, heard what they were saying. He wanted to save Joseph from his brothers and said, Let us not kill him. Throw him in that pit and leave him in the wilderness. Let us shed no blood!—for he wanted to save him and bring him home to his father.

And it happened when Joseph came to his brothers that they tore his coat of many colors from his back and threw him in the pit—and it was dry. There was no water in the pit.

And so they sat down and ate their supper and raised their eyes and look! A caravan of Ishmaelites came, with their camels loaded with precious spices, balsam, and myrrh, on their way down to Egypt.

Judah said, What good is it to kill the boy and cover up his blood? He is our brother—our own flesh. Let's sell him to the Ishmaelites, and we'll not lay a hand on him.

The brothers agreed, and when the Ishmaelites came by, they pulled Joseph out of the pit and sold him for twenty pieces of silver, and the merchants took Joseph down to Egypt with them.

Now Reuben came back and saw that Joseph was not in the pit, and tore his clothes, and went to his brothers and said, The child is gone! And I—what am I going to do?

And the brothers took Joseph's coat of many colors, slaughtered a goat and dipped the coat into the blood, and brought it to their father and said, Look what we have found. Do you know if this is your son's coat or not?

Jacob knew the coat of many colors and said, This is my son's coat! An evil beast has devoured him! Torn! Torn in pieces is my son! And Jacob tore his clothes and put on sackcloth and mourned his son. All his sons and daughters came to comfort him, but he would not be comforted and said, I will go down to my grave mourning for my son Joseph! That is how Joseph's father wept for him.

But the merchants took Joseph down to Egypt and sold him to Potiphar.

And the Lord was with Joseph, and everything he did went well. He lived in the house of his Egyptian master, and Potiphar saw that the Lord was with Joseph, and Joseph prospered in everything he did. Potiphar liked Joseph and made Joseph his attendant and put Joseph in charge of all his household and of everything he owned, and from that day everything prospered. The Lord blessed everything the Egyptian owned at home and in the field, for Joseph's sake. And the Egyptian left everything in Joseph's care, and he himself did nothing but eat and drink.

Now Joseph was a beautiful young man and well built, and his master's wife looked at him and said, Come, lie with me.

But Joseph would not and said, You know my master has put all his household and everything he owns into my hands. He himself is no greater in his own house than he has made me. He denies me nothing except you, because you are his wife. How could I sin against God and do such a wicked thing!

Day in and day out she urged Joseph to be with her and lie with her, but he would not.

It happened, one day, that he went into the house

to see to his work, and there were no servants in the room. Potiphar's wife took hold of Joseph's coat and said, Lie with me. But Joseph left his coat in her hand and ran out of the house, and she screamed for the servants and said, You see what this Hebrew my husband has brought into the house has done! He makes nothing but trouble! He came in here and wanted to lie with me, but I screamed and he ran out of the house. This is his coat!

When her husband came home she told him the same story and said, You see what that Hebrew slave you brought into this house has done to me!

Potiphar burned with anger and took Joseph and threw him into the prison house where they put Pharaoh's prisoners, and Joseph remained there in prison.

But the Lord was with Joseph, and the warden of the prison liked him and put him in charge of all the prisoners. Anything that needed to be done in the prison had to be done through Joseph. Now that the warden had Joseph do everything, he needed to do nothing at all! And the Lord was with Joseph, and everything he did prospered.

Two years passed, and Pharaoh dreamed that he stood by the Nile and saw seven fine, fat cows come out of the water and graze among the reeds on the meadow. Then seven more cows came out of the water, but they were ugly and thin, and they went to stand beside the fine, fat cows on the banks of the Nile. And the ugly, thin cows swallowed up the seven fine, fat cows. And Pharaoh woke.

He fell asleep again, and again he dreamed, and saw seven ears of grain, healthy and full, growing out of one stalk. Then there sprouted seven ears of grain that were thin and scorched by the east wind. The thin ears of grain swallowed up the healthy, full ears. And Pharaoh woke and knew it was a dream.

When morning came he was troubled. He sent for his magicians and all the wise men of Egypt and told them his dreams, but there was not one who could interpret his dreams for him.

Now the chief cupbearer said, This is the day to put me in mind of my sins! That time when Pharaoh was angry and threw me and the chief baker in prison, we each had a dream in the very same night. There was a young Hebrew in the prison with us. He interpreted our dreams, and each dream meant something different, and everything turned out as he had said: I was returned to my post, and the other was hanged.

And Pharaoh sent for Joseph, and Joseph was quickly brought out of the prison. They cut his hair and changed his clothes and brought him before Pharaoh.

Pharaoh said, I have had a dream, and there is no one who can interpret it. They tell me that you know how to interpret dreams.

Joseph said, It is not up to me, but God, who will show Pharaoh His favor.

Pharaoh said, I dreamed that I stood by the Nile and saw seven fine, fat cows come out of the water and graze among the reeds in the meadow. Then I saw seven more cows, and they were skinny and lean and ugly, and they came out of the water; nowhere in all of Egypt have I ever seen such ugly cows. And the seven lean, ugly cows swallowed up the first seven fine, fat cows, and no one would have known that they had eaten them: they were as ugly and skinny as ever. Then I woke.

Again I slept, and I had another dream. I saw seven ears of grain, healthy and full, growing out of one stalk. Then there sprouted seven ears of grain that were thin and scorched by the east wind, and the seven thin ears swallowed up the full ears. I have told my wise men, and they don't know what it means.

Joseph said, Pharaoh's two dreams mean the same thing. God has made known to Pharaoh what is to come. The seven fine cows mean seven years, and the seven good ears of grain mean the same seven years of abundance; it is one and the same dream. The seven ugly, lean cows that step out of the water are seven years, and the seven thin, scorched ears of corn are the same seven years of famine. There will be seven abundant years throughout the land of Egypt, followed by seven years of famine, and the seven years of famine will ravage the land so that no one will remember the seven abundant years. Hunger will be so great that the abundance will be forgotten. Because Pharaoh has dreamed the same dream twice, it means that God is sure to do all this and soon.

And Joseph said, Now let Pharaoh find a man who is wise and capable and put him in charge of the land of Egypt. Let him make sure that there shall be governors in every part of the land who will take a fifth part of the harvest of the seven abundant years and store the grain in Pharaoh's storehouses for the use of the cities during the seven years of famine that will come upon Egypt, or the country will be ravaged by hunger.

The plan seemed good to Pharaoh and to his court, and Pharaoh said, Where shall we find another man in whom the spirit of God speaks as He speaks in this man? Because God has made all these things known to you, there is no one so full of understanding and wisdom as you. You shall have charge over my palace, and all my people shall obey you. Only inasmuch as I sit on the throne shall I be greater than you.

Pharaoh took the ring from his finger and put it on Joseph's finger. He gave him robes of precious linen and put a golden chain around his neck and made him ride in the chariot of his second in command, and they ran ahead of Joseph crying, Bow down, for Pharaoh has put Egypt under the charge of this man!

And Pharaoh said to Joseph, I am Pharaoh, but without you no one lifts a hand or a foot in all the land of Egypt.

For seven abundant years the land produced plentifully. Joseph collected the harvests of those seven years and stored them. In each city he stored the food that grew in the fields round about. Joseph heaped up such a quantity of grain he had to stop keeping count, for the quantity was measureless as the sands of the sea.

The seven abundant years came to an end in Egypt, and the seven years of famine began, as Joseph had foretold. And there was famine in all the lands round about. Only in Egypt was there bread to eat. When the Egyptians were hungry and came to Pharaoh crying for bread, Pharaoh said, Go to Joseph and do what he says.

And now Joseph opened the storehouses and sold the grain to the Egyptians, and the longer the famine lasted, the more severe it became, and the whole world came to Egypt to buy grain from Joseph, for the famine was terrible everywhere.

Now when Jacob heard that there was grain to be had in Egypt, he said to his sons, Why do you stand there looking at one another? Go down to Egypt and buy us some grain so that we can live and not die.

He did not send Joseph's little brother Benjamin with them, because he was afraid of what might happen to him.

The famine was severe in Canaan. Jacob's sons were among many people traveling down to Egypt. Joseph sold grain to everyone who came, and Joseph's brothers came and stood before him and bowed their faces to the ground. Joseph knew they were his brothers and remembered the dreams that he had dreamed, but he acted as if they were strangers and spoke roughly to them and said, Where are you from?

They said, We have come from Canaan to buy grain. They didn't know it was Joseph.

Joseph said, Spies—that's what you are! You've come to spy out the weakness of this land!

They answered, No, my lord! We are your lordship's servants and have come to buy grain. We are brothers, the sons of one man, and are honest men. We are not spies!

Joseph said, No! The weakness of the land is what you've come to spy out.

They said, My lord, there are twelve of us, sons of one man, who lives in Canaan. The youngest is home with his father, and there was another brother, but he's no longer here.

Joseph said, And I say you're spies! I will put you to the test. One of you go home and get this youngest brother about whom you have told me. Bring him here. The rest of you can wait in prison. As Pharaoh lives, you're not leaving here unless you bring me your youngest brother and I see that the story you have told me is the truth. If not, as Pharaoh lives, you're spies and you shall die! And he put all of them in prison for three days.

On the third day Joseph said to them, Do what I say and no harm shall come to you. I am a God-fearing man. Prove to me that you are honest men. Leave one of your brothers here in prison. The rest of you go home. Take back the grain you have bought to feed your hungry families and bring me your youngest brother. Then I'll believe the story you have told me. If not, you shall die.

And they complied, but they said, one to the other, Our guilt has found us out because of Joseph. We saw his soul's anguish when he pleaded with us, and we would not listen! That's why this misery has come upon us!

Reuben said, Didn't I tell you not to harm the child? You wouldn't listen to me. Now we are paying for his blood.

They did not know that Joseph understood what they were saying, because he spoke with them through an interpreter, and Joseph turned away from them and wept. Then he turned back and he took Simeon and had him bound before their eyes.

Now Joseph ordered their bags to be filled with grain and had each man's money put back into the mouth of his bag. Joseph's brothers loaded their bags onto their asses and went on their way.

Now when they stopped for the night, one of them opened his bag to feed his ass and there was his money, lying in the mouth of his bag! He said, My money has got back into my bag!

Their hearts sank. They trembled and looked at one another and said, What is God doing to us!

They came home to their father Jacob, in Canaan, and told him what had happened. They said, The man who is the lord of Egypt spoke harshly to us and thought that we were spies. We said, We are not spies! We are honest men, twelve brothers, the sons of one father. One brother is no longer here, and the youngest is home with his father. But the man said, Prove to me that you are honest men. Leave one of your brothers here, take back as much grain as you need for your households, and go home, but bring me back your youngest brother. Then I shall know you are not spies but honest men, and I'll give you back your brother and you'll be free to trade in Egypt.

And now they opened their bags and each one found his purse full of money in the mouth of his bag and they were frightened, and Jacob was frightened. He said, You rob me of one child after another! Joseph is no longer here and Simeon is no longer here and now you want to take Benjamin. Everything goes against me!

Reuben said, Put Benjamin under my care. If I don't bring the boy back, you can put my two sons to death! I pledge myself for him.

But Jacob said, My son is not going to Egypt with you. His brother is dead and he is the only one left—if something happened to him on the way, it would bring my gray head down to the grave with sorrow.

But the famine was bitter in Canaan, and when they had eaten up the grain from Egypt, their father said, Go back and buy more food.

Now Judah said, The man made it clear he will not

see us unless our brother comes with us. If you let Benjamin come, we will go down and buy you some food to eat. If you don't let him go, we won't go back, because the man will not see us.

Jacob said, You did me an evil turn when you told the man you had another brother! Why did you tell him?

They said, Because he questioned us and asked us about ourselves and our family. He asked us, Is your father still alive? How many brothers are you? We answered his questions. How could we know he would say, Bring your brother back with you.

Judah said, Let the boy go with me, in my care, so that we can go and get food for you and for us and for our little ones, so that we can live and not die. I pledge myself for the boy. If I don't bring him back and set him here before you, the guilt be upon my head my life long. We've waited so long, we could have gone and returned twice over.

Their father said, If it must be so, then take with you the best fruits of this land and bring the man gifts—a little balsam and some honey, spices and myrrh, nuts and almonds. Take money, and take back the money you found in your bags. Perhaps there was some mistake. Yes, and take your brother. Go back to the man. May God Almighty make him merciful to you and give you back your brother Simeon and let you bring Benjamin back! As for me, if I must lose my child I must lose him!

And so they took the gifts and twice the sums of

money, and they took Benjamin with them and set out for Egypt. And they came and stood before Joseph, and Joseph saw they had brought Benjamin with them and he said to his steward, Take them to my house. Slaughter an animal and cook it. These men will eat their midday meal with me.

The steward did as Joseph said, but the men were afraid and said, one to the other, it's because of the money we found in our bags last time. That's why they're taking us to his house—so they can fall on us and make us their slaves and take our asses!

They stopped the steward at the entrance of the house and said, Sir, if you please, we came down once before, to buy grain, and when we stopped for the night and opened our bags, each of us found his money, in the exact weight, right in the mouth of his bag, and so we have brought it back with us. And we have brought more money to buy grain. We don't know how the money got back into our bags.

The man said, It's all right. Don't worry. Your God, and the God of your father, put your purses back into your bags. I received your payment in full.

And he brought Simeon out to them and took them into the house and gave them water to bathe their feet and fodder for their asses. And they made their presents ready, for they had heard they were to eat their midday meal in Joseph's house.

Joseph entered the room and they gave him their

presents and bowed down to the ground before him. He greeted them and said, And how old is the man your father, about whom you told me? Is he still alive?

They said, Our father is alive and is well, your lordship. And they bowed down to the ground. Joseph looked at his brother Benjamin, his own mother's son, and said, So this is the youngest brother about whom you told me. May the Lord be merciful to you, my son.

And Joseph said nothing more and hurried from the room. His heart yearned with love for his younger brother, and he looked for a place where he could weep and went into his chamber and wept, and then he washed his face and returned to them and, keeping his feelings in check, said, You may serve the meal.

They served him, where he sat by himself, and the Egyptians ate by themselves, because it was an abomination to the Egyptians to eat at the same table with Hebrews. But Joseph's brothers they seated in the order of their birth, from the firstborn to the youngest, so that they looked at one another in astonishment. They were served from Joseph's own table, and Benjamin's portion was five times as large as any of the others; and they ate and drank in good spirits.

Now Joseph instructed his steward and said, Fill each man's bag with as much grain as he can carry, and put each man's full purse back into the mouth of his bag. Put my silver cup in the mouth of the bag of the youngest, along with his grain and his money. And the man did what Joseph said. In the morning when it became light, they sent the brothers off with their asses, and they left the city.

They had not gone far when Joseph said to his steward, Go after those men. When you catch up with them, say, Why do you repay kindness with evil? Why have you taken my master's silver cup out of which he drinks and which he uses for divinations? What a wicked thing to do!

And the steward pursued Joseph's brothers and caught up with them and repeated Joseph's words to them. They said, Why does your lordship say such things to us? We would never do such a thing! Didn't we bring back the money we found in our bags? Why would we steal your lord's silver and gold out of his house? If you find it on any one of us, that one shall die, and the rest of us will be your lordship's slaves!

He said, Very well, but only he in whose bag the thing is found shall be his slave; the rest of you will be free to go.

Each one quickly lowered his bag to the ground and opened his bag, and the steward made his search beginning with the eldest and ending with the youngest, and he found the cup in Benjamin's bag.

And now they tore their clothes and reloaded their asses, and so they came back to the city.

The steward took them to Joseph's house, and they

threw themselves down before him with their faces to the ground.

Joseph said, How could you do such a thing? Don't you know I am a man who divines the truth?

Judah said, My lord, what can we say? How can we prove our innocence? God has found out your servants' crime. We and the boy in whose sack the cup was found are your lordship's slaves.

Joseph said, I would not be so unjust. Only he who had my cup shall be my slave. The rest of you go home to your father.

Now Judah stepped before him. He said, My lord, allow your servant to speak a word in your lordship's ear, and do not be angry with your servant, you who have the greatness of Pharaoh himself! The first time your servants came before your lordship, you questioned us and asked if we had a father and brothers. We told your lordship we had a father and that he was old, and that we had a little brother born to my father's old age, and another brother who is dead, and only this one boy is left of his mother's sons, and his father loves him.

Your lordship said to your servants, Bring me the boy, and I will be gracious to him! We told your lordship, If the boy leaves his father, his father will die! But your lordship said, Unless your brother comes with you, you shall not see my face! We went home to our father and told him your lordship's words. Our father said, Go back and buy us some more food! But we said, We cannot go.

The man will not see us unless our youngest brother comes with us! Our father said, You know my wife bore me two sons in my old age. One is gone, and I told myself an animal had torn my son—torn him to pieces—and I never saw his face again! Now you want to take this child away from me!

And so I pledged myself to our father for the boy's safety and said, If I don't bring the boy back to you, I shall bear the guilt my life long! Therefore let me remain and be your lordship's slave in the boy's stead. Let the child go home with his brothers, for how can I go home and witness my father's sorrow and bear to see grief bring his gray head down to the grave.

Now Joseph could not control himself any longer in front of all his servants and cried, Get everybody out of here! And so no one was by when Joseph made himself known to his brothers and wept so loudly the Egyptians could hear him and Pharaoh's household was told of it.

Joseph said, I am Joseph! Is my father still alive?

The brothers could not answer, they were so horrified in his presence. But Joseph said, Won't you come closer to me?

And they came closer, and he said, I am Joseph, your brother, whom you sold into Egypt! Don't grieve, and don't be frightened of my anger because you sold me here, to this place. It was God who sent me ahead to save your lives. The famine has lasted two years, and it will be another five years before there will be any plowing or reaping. God sent me to prepare a great salvation for you and your children and your children's children on the earth.

It was not you, it was the Lord, who sent me here to be a father to Pharaoh and a steward of his household, and to govern all the land of Egypt. Hurry home to my father and say, Your son Joseph says, God has made me lord over the land of Egypt. Come to me! Hurry! You shall live in the land of Goshen where I can be near you and can provide for you and your children and your children's children, your flocks and herds and all you have, because there are five years of famine yet to come.

And he said to them, It is true! It is me! It is me your eyes, and my brother Benjamin's eyes, are seeing! It is my mouth speaking to you. Go tell my father and bring him to me. Hurry!

And he threw his arms around his brother Benjamin and wept, and Benjamin wept on his brother Joseph's neck. And Joseph kissed all his brothers and wept with them, and now his brothers could talk with him.

The news reached Pharaoh's palace: Joseph's brothers have come to Egypt! And it pleased Pharaoh and his court. Pharaoh said, Tell your brothers all that is best in Egypt shall be theirs; they shall live on the fat of the land! And Joseph gave each of his brothers a splendid robe, but to Benjamin he gave three hundred silver pieces and five robes. And for his father he sent ten asses loaded with the best things of Egypt, and ten she-asses loaded with grain. To his brothers he said, You are not to quarrel among yourselves along the way!

And they left Egypt and came home to their father in Canaan and told him, Joseph is alive! He is the man who rules over all the land of Egypt.

But Jacob's heart was numb; he did not believe them. They told him everything Joseph had said to them, and when he saw the carriages sent to carry him to Egypt, Jacob's spirit lifted. And they went down to Egypt, Jacob and his children and his children's children. There were in all seventy persons in Jacob's household, who went to Egypt with him.

And Joseph put horses to his carriage and came out to meet his father, and when he saw him he threw his arms around his father and wept long upon his neck.

And Jacob said, Now I can die, for I have seen your face and know that you are alive!

GREEN SONG

May Sarton

Here where nothing passes,
Where centuries have stayed
Alive under the grasses,
Gently the heart is laid.

Oh, breathe these meadows in
Till you are filled with green,
A drunkard of the scene
Your dreams will wander in.

Then set the eyes to graze,
Set urban eyes to browse
These rich, brief summer days
Among the trees and cows.

And sleep away all care,
Lay rushing time to rest,
And rise up light as air,
Green-fed and meadow-blessed.

AN OLD-FASHIONED SONG

John Hollander

No more walks in the wood:
The trees have all been cut
Down, and where once they stood
Not even a wagon rut
Appears along the path
Low brush is taking over.

No more walks in the wood . . .
This is the aftermath
Of afternoons in the clover
Fields where we once made love
Then wandered home together
Where the trees arched above.
There, we made our own weather
When branches were the sky.
Now they are gone for good,
And you, too, and now I
Am only a passer-by.

We and the trees and the way
Back from the fields of play
Lasted as long as we could.
No more walks in the wood.

ON THE LINE

◄§ *Vesle Fenstermaker*

in the untouched landscape
the primal ape
perusing grubs
digs into a rotten log
with a small stick

in the whole earth
there is no metal
no plastic   no wire
no fabric   no glass

yet in the moment
when his thumb
meets his finger
around the stick

the first blue Chevy
begins

ONE MOMENT

◦§ *Vesle Fenstermaker*

The boy stares at the flat circle.
"Big hand, little hand," says his mother.
"Tick, tick. Like this. You see?
Around and around. It measures."

His eyes follow her hand.
The clock face enters him.

This instant,
Nameless an instant ago,
Becomes 4:27.

He knows
Now is a minute
With fifty-nine brothers,
His to muster and march.
They make the day
And its dark opposite.

Now he will live by ticks,
Out of the drift,
The frightening flow.

Sheltered, enclosed,
Caged.

THE MOUSE WHOSE NAME IS TIME

◄§ Robert Francis

The Mouse whose name is Time
Is out of sound and sight.
He nibbles at the day
And nibbles at the night.

He nibbles at the summer
Till all of it is gone.
He nibbles at the seashore.
He nibbles at the moon.

Yet no man not a seer,
No woman not a sibyl
Can ever ever hear
Or see him nibble, nibble.

And whence or how he comes
And how or where he goes
Nobody dead remembers,
Nobody living knows.

LINES AT THE NEW YEAR

⋖§ Donald Justice

The old year slips past
    unseen, the way a snake goes.

Vanishes,
    and the grass closes behind it.

THE WRITER IN THE FAMILY

*Adapted by E. L. Doctorow
from his story "The Writer in the Family"*

In 1955 my father died while his mother was still alive in a nursing home. The old lady was ninety and hadn't even known he was ill. Thinking the shock might kill her, my aunts told her that he had moved to Arizona for his bronchitis. To my grandmother, Arizona was like the Alps; it was where you went for your health. That is, it was where you went if you had the money. Since my father had failed in every business he had ever tried, this was the part of the news my grandmother dwelled on. Her son had finally had some success. And so it came about that as we mourned his death, my grandmother was bragging to her cronies about her son's new life in the dry air of the desert.

My aunts had decided to spare my grandmother without consulting us. It meant that my mother, my brother, and I could not visit Grandma because we were supposed to have moved to Arizona too. We were a family, after all. My brother Harold and I didn't mind—it was always a nightmare at the old people's home, where they all sat around staring at us while we tried to make conversation with Grandma. She had many complaints, and her mind wandered. Not seeing her was no disappointment, either, for my mother, who had never gotten along with the old woman and did not visit her when she could have.

But what was disturbing was that my aunts had acted, as that side of the family always had, making government on everyone's behalf, they being the true citizens by blood, we the lesser citizens by marriage. It was this attitude that had tormented my mother all her married life. She claimed Jack's family had never accepted her. She had battled them for twenty-five years as an outsider.

A month after the funeral, my aunt Frances phoned us from her home in Larchmont. Aunt Frances was the wealthier of my father's sisters. Her husband was a lawyer, and both her sons were away at college. She had called to say that Grandma was asking why she didn't hear from Jack. I had answered the phone. "You're the writer in the family," my aunt said. "Your father had so much faith in you. Would you mind making up something? Send it to me, and I'll read it to her. She won't know the difference."

That evening, at the kitchen table, I pushed my homework aside and began a letter. I tried to imagine my father's response to his new life. He had never been west. He had never traveled anywhere. In his generation, the great journey was from the working class to the professional class. He hadn't managed that, either. But he loved New York, where he had been born and lived his life, and he was always discovering new things about it. He especially loved the old parts of the city: the docks below Canal Street, where he would find ship's outfitters or firms that imported spices and teas. He was a salesman for an appliance wholesaler with accounts all over the city. He liked to bring home rare cheeses or strange foreign vegetables that were sold only in certain neighborhoods. Once he brought home an antique ship's telescope in a wooden case with a brass snap.

"Dear Mama," I wrote. "Arizona is beautiful. The sun shines all day and the air is warm and I feel better than I have in years. The desert is not as barren as you would expect, but filled with wildflowers and cactus trees that look like men holding their arms out. You can see great distances in whatever direction you turn. To the west is a range of mountains maybe fifty miles from here, but in the morning with the sun on them you can see the snow on their crests."

My aunt Frances called a few days later to say that as she read my letter aloud to the old lady in the nursing home, the full effect of Jack's death had come over her. She had left the room and gone out to the parking lot to cry. "I wept so," she said. "I felt such a terrible longing for him. You're so right—he loved to travel, he loved life, he loved everything."

We began trying to organize our lives. My father had borrowed money against his insurance policy, and there was very little left. There was a couple of thousand dollars in a savings bank that had to be kept there until the estate was settled. Our lawyer was Aunt Frances's husband, and he was very proper. "The estate!" my mother cried, her hands clutching the sides of her head, as if to pull out her hair. "The estate!"

We lived in an apartment on the corner of 175th Street and the Grand Concourse, one flight up. Three rooms. I shared the bedroom with my brother. It was jammed with furniture, because when my father needed a hospital bed in the last weeks of his illness, we had moved some of the front-room pieces into the bedroom and made over the living room for him. My mother continued to sleep on the living room sofa that had been their bed before his illness. The two rooms were connected by a narrow hall made even narrower by bookcases along the wall. Off the hall was a small kitchen and also a dinette and a bathroom.

There were lots of appliances in the kitchen—broiler, toaster, blender, pressure cooker—that my father had gotten at cost. Treasured words in our house: "at cost." But most of them went unused, because my mother had her own ways and did not care for them. They were in part responsible for the awful clutter of our lives, and now she wanted to get rid of them. "We're being buried," she said. "Who needs them!"

So we agreed to throw out or sell anything we weren't using. While I found boxes for the appliances and my brother tied up the boxes, my mother opened my father's closet and took out his clothes. He'd had several suits because, as a salesman, he had to look his best. My mother wanted us to try on his suits to see which of them could be altered and used. My brother refused to try them on. I tried on one jacket, which was too large for me. The lining inside the sleeves chilled my arms, and a faint sense of my father's presence came over me.

"This is way too big," I said.

"Don't worry," my mother said. "I had it cleaned. Would I let you wear it if I hadn't?"

It was evening, the end of winter, and snow was coming down on the windowsill and melting as it settled. The ceiling bulb glared on a pile of my father's suits and trousers flung across the bed in the shape of a dead man. We refused to try on anything more, and my mother began to cry.

"What are you crying for?" my brother shouted. "You wanted to get rid of things, didn't you?"

A few weeks later, my aunt phoned again and said she thought it would be necessary to have another letter from Jack. Grandma had fallen out of her chair and was very depressed.

"How long does this go on?" my mother said.

"It's not so terrible," my aunt said, "for the little time she has left to make things easier for her."

My mother slammed down the phone. "He can't even die when he wants to!" she cried. "Even death comes second to Mama! What are they afraid of—the shock will kill her? Nothing can kill her. A stake through the heart couldn't kill her!"

I sat down in the kitchen to write the letter. It was more difficult than the first one. "Don't watch me," I said to my brother. "It's hard enough."

"Dear Mama," I wrote. "I hope you're feeling well. We're all fit as a fiddle. The life here is good, and the people are very friendly and informal. Nobody wears suits and ties here. Just a pair of slacks and a short-sleeved shirt. Perhaps a sweater in the evening. I have bought into a very successful radio and record business, and I'm doing well. You remember Jack's Electric, my old place on Forty-third Street? Well, now it's Jack's Arizona Electric, and we have a line of television sets as well."

I sent the letter off to Aunt Frances, and as we all knew she would, she phoned soon after. My brother held his hand over the receiver. "It's Frances with her latest review," he said.

"Jonathan? You're a very talented young man. I just wanted to tell you what a blessing your letter was. Grandma's whole face lit up when I read her the part about Jack's new store. That would be an excellent way to continue."

"Well, I hope I don't have to do this anymore, Aunt Frances. It's not very honest."

Her tone changed. "Is your mother there? Let me talk to her."

"She's not here," I said.

"You tell her not to worry," my aunt said. "A poor old lady who has never wished anything but the best for her will soon die."

I did not repeat this for my mother to add to her collection of unforgivable family remarks. But then I had to live with it myself, and with the possible truth it might contain. Each side defended its position with exaggerated claims, but I, who only wanted peace, took no stands, like my father himself.

Years ago, my father's life had fallen into a pattern of business failures and missed opportunities. The great debate between his family, on the one side, and my mother, Ruth, on the other, was this: who was responsible for the fact that he had not lived up to anyone's expectations?

When spring came, as my mother had predicted, Grandma was still alive. One Sunday, my mother and brother and I took the bus to New Jersey to visit my father's grave, which was planted with tiny shoots of evergreen but lacked a headstone. We had chosen one and paid for it, and then the stonecutters had gone on strike. Without a headstone, my father didn't seem to me properly buried. My mother's gaze wandered over the family headstones. "They were always too fine for other people," she said. "Even in the old days on Stanton Street. They put on airs. Nobody was ever good enough for them. Finally, Jack himself was not good enough for them. Except for getting them things at cost. *Then* he was good enough for them."

"Mom, please," my brother said.

"If I had known. Before I ever met him he was tied to his mother's apron strings. And Essie's apron strings were like chains. We had to live where we could be near them for the Sunday visits. Every Sunday that was my life, a visit to Mama. Whatever she knew I wanted—a better apartment, a stick of furniture, summer camp for you boys—she spoke against it. And nothing changed. Nothing ever changed." She began to cry.

Somewhere during this time I began dreaming of my father. Not the handsome father of my childhood, with healthy pink skin, brown eyes, and hair parted in the middle. I dreamed of my father come back from the dead. Death had terribly damaged him. He was very yellowed, spoiled and unclean, and he might soon die again. His entire personality was changed. He was angry and impatient with all of us, although we were trying to help him. We were struggling to get him home, but something always prevented us. His clothes, which had become too large for him, had caught in the car door; or else he was all bandaged, and as we tried to lift him into his wheelchair, the bandages began to unroll and catch in the wheels. My mother looked on, tried to reason with him, tried to get him to cooperate.

The dream made me feel guilty. I felt guilty *in* the dream too, because it was understood by all of us that he was to live alone. We were trying to take him someplace where he would live by himself, until he died again. That was the dream. I shared it with no one. Once when I woke, crying out, my brother turned on the light. He wanted to know what I had been dreaming, but I pretended I didn't remember.

I became so fearful of this dream that I tried not to go to sleep. I tried to think of good things about my father and to remember him before his illness. He used to call me "matey." "Hello, matey," he would say when he came home from work. He always wanted us to go someplace—to the store, to the park, to a ball game. He loved to walk. When I went walking with him, he would say: "Hold your shoulders back, don't slump. Hold your head up and look at the world. Walk as if you meant it!" As he strode down the street, he moved with a bounce; his shoulders moved from side to side. He was always eager to see what was around the corner.

Aunt Frances's next request for a letter came at a special time: my brother Harold had met a girl he liked and had gone out with her several times. Now she was coming to our house for dinner.

We had prepared for days, cleaning everything in sight, washing the dust from the tall glasses and good dishes. Mother came home from work early to get the dinner going. We opened the folding table in the living room and brought in the kitchen chairs. My mother spread the table with a fresh white cloth and put out her silver. It was the first family occasion since my father's illness.

I liked my brother's girlfriend a lot. She was a thin girl with very straight hair, and she had a terrific smile. Her presence seemed to excite the air. It was amazing to have a living, breathing girl in the house. She looked around, and what she said was: "Oh, I've never seen so many books!" While she and my brother sat at the table, my mother was in the kitchen putting food into serving bowls and I was going from the kitchen to the living room, kidding around like a waiter, with a white cloth over my arm and a high style of service, sweeping the serving dish of green beans onto the table. In the kitchen, my mother's eyes were sparkling. She looked at me and nodded as her mouth shaped the words "She's adorable!"

My brother let himself be waited on. He was uneasy about what we might say or do. He kept glancing at the girl to see how things were going. She worked in an insurance office and was taking a course in accounting at City College. Harold was under a terrible strain, but he was excited and happy too. He had bought a bottle of wine to go with the roast chicken. He held up his glass and proposed a toast. My mother said: "To good health and happiness," and we all drank. At this moment the phone rang, and I went into the bedroom to get it.

"Jonathan? This is your aunt Frances. How is everyone?"

"Fine, thank you."

"I want to ask one last favor of you. I need a letter

from Jack. Your grandma's very ill. Do you think you can?"

"Who is it?" my mother called from the living room.

"Okay, Aunt Frances," I said quickly. "I have to go now; we're eating dinner." And I hung up the phone.

"It was my friend Louie," I said, sitting back down. "He didn't know the math pages to review."

The dinner was very fine. Harold and Susan washed the dishes, and by the time they were done, my mother and I had folded up the table and put it back against the wall, and I had swept the crumbs up with the carpet sweeper. We all sat and talked and listened to records for a while, and then my brother took Susan home. The evening had gone very well.

Once, when my mother wasn't home, my brother had pointed out something to me. The letters from Jack weren't really necessary. "What is all this!" he said, holding his palms up. "Grandma is almost totally blind, she's half deaf and half dead. Does this situation really call for your literary compositions? Would the old lady know the difference if someone read her the phone book?"

"Then why does Frances ask for them?"

"That is the question, Jonathan. Why does she? After all, she could write the letters herself—what difference would it make? And if not Frances, why not her sons, the college boys? They should have learned to write by now."

"But they're not Jack's sons," I said.

"That's exactly the point," my brother said. "The idea is *service*. Dad used to bust his balls getting them things wholesale, getting them deals on things. Does Lady Frances of Larchmont really need things at cost? And Aunt Molly? And Aunt Molly's husband and Aunt Molly's ex-husband? Even Grandma? Dad was always on the hook for something. They never thought his time was important. They never figured out that every favor he got for them was one he had to pay back. They want appliances, watches, china, opera tickets, any goddamn thing? Call Jack."

"It was a matter of pride to him to be able to do those things," I said, "to show them he had connections."

"Yeah?" my brother said. "I wonder why." He looked out the window and then back at me. "Think about it," he said.

Yet I had agreed once again to write a letter from the desert, and so I did. I mailed it off to Aunt Frances. A few days later, when I came home from school, I saw her sitting in her car in front of our house. She drove a black Buick Roadmaster with whitewall tires. She blew the horn when she saw me. I went over and leaned in at the window.

"Hello, Jonathan," she said. "I haven't long. Can you get in the car?"

"Mom's not home," I said. "She's working."

"I know that. I came to talk to you. Can you get in the car for a moment, please?"

I got in the car. My aunt Frances was a very pretty woman, very elegant in her expensive clothes. She wore white gloves, and she held the steering wheel and looked straight ahead as she talked, as if we were in traffic and not sitting at the curb.

"Jonathan," she said, "there is your letter on the seat. Needless to say, I didn't read it to Grandma. I'm giving it back to you, and I won't ever say a word to anyone. I never expected this from you. I never thought you were capable of doing something so deliberately cruel."

I said nothing.

"Your mother has bitter feelings and now I see that she has poisoned you with them. She has always resented the family. She is a very strong-willed, selfish person."

"No she isn't," I said.

"I wouldn't expect you to agree. She drove poor Jack crazy with her demands. If he happened to make a little money he had to buy Ruth a mink jacket because she was desperate to have one. He had debts to pay but she wanted mink. My brother should have accomplished something special. But he loved your mother and he spent his life trying to satisfy her, while all she ever thought about was keeping up with the Joneses. I'm sorry to have to speak like this," Aunt Frances said. "If I have nothing good to say about someone, I'd rather say nothing." After a moment she said more softly: "How are you all getting along?"

"Fine."

"I would invite you up for Passover if I thought your mother would accept."

I didn't answer.

She turned on the engine. "I'll say goodbye now, Jonathan. Take your letter. I hope you'll think about what you've done."

That evening when my mother came home from work I saw that she wasn't as pretty as my Aunt Frances. I saw now that she was too heavy and that her hair had no style.

"Why are you looking at me?" she said.

"I'm not."

"I learned something interesting today," my mother said. "We may be entitled to a pension for the time your father was in the Navy."

That took me by surprise. Nobody had ever told me my father was in the Navy.

"He was training to be an officer," she went on, "but the war ended and he never got his commission."

After dinner we went through my father's papers

looking for proof of his years of service. We came up with two things, a Victory medal, which my brother said everyone got for being in the service during World War I, and a photograph of my father and his shipmates in bell-bottomed trousers on the deck of a ship.

"I never knew this," I found myself saying. "I never knew this."

I took the picture of my father and his shipmates and propped it against the lamp at my bedside. I looked into his youthful face and tried to see in it the Father I knew. I looked at the picture a long time. Only gradually did my eye connect it to the set of Great Sea Novels in the bottom shelf of the bookcase a few feet away. My father had given that set to me and it included books by Herman Melville, Joseph Conrad, Victor Hugo, and Captain Marryat. And lying across the top of the books, jammed in under the shelf above, was his old ship's telescope in its wooden case with the brass snap.

I thought how stupid, how blind I had been not to have understood until now what my father's dream for his life had been.

However, in reading over my last letter from Arizona—the one that had so angered Aunt Frances—I see that he had conveyed some sense of his longing to me, the writer in the family. This is the letter.

Dear Mama,

This will be my final letter to you since I have been told by the doctors that I am dying.

I have sold my store at a very fine profit and am sending Frances a check for five thousand dollars to be deposited in your account. My present to you, Mama dear. Let Frances show you the passbook.

As for my illness, the doctors haven't told me what it is, but I know that I am simply dying of the wrong life. I should never have come to the desert. It wasn't the place for me.

I have asked Ruth and the boys to have my body cremated and the ashes scattered in the ocean.

Your loving son,

Jack

BOOK THREE *Words on the Page,*

GRAY SQUIRREL
◄§ Robert Francis

Flighty as birds, fluid as fishes
He flies, he floats through boughs, he flashes,
Almost before he starts he finishes.
As rain runs silver down a tree
He runs straight up quicksilverly.
He whizzes, he somersaults, he whirls
Like a plurality of squirrels
    Then suddenly sits
    With all his wits.
How could I catch him, how can I match him
Except with a fast eye and my best wishes?

A CURIOSITY

Karl Shapiro

Tiny bees come to see what I am,
Lying in the sun at summer's end,
Writing a poem on a reclining chair.
A butterfly approaches and retreats,
Flies bang into my body by mistake,
And tinier things I can't identify;
And now and then a slow gigantic wasp
Rows on its stately voyage to the fence.
The trees are still too little to have birds;
Besides, the neighbors all have special cats
Bred for their oddity or arrogance.
A dragonfly sips at a lemon twig
After a helicopter landing. It
Appears that I am a curiosity
In my own backyard.
The dog of doubtful breed
Sleeps on the carpet of the sod,
And a bee necks with a rose.

EXEUNT
◆§ Richard Wilbur

Piecemeal the summer dies;
At the field's edge a daisy lives alone;
  A last shawl of burning lies
    On a gray field stone.

All cries are thin and terse;
The field has droned the summer's final mass;
  A cricket like a dwindled hearse
    Crawls from the dry grass.

A MILKWEED SPEAKS

From "Two Voices in a Meadow" by Richard Wilbur

Anonymous as cherubs
Over the crib of God,
White seeds are floating
Out of my burst pod.
What power had I
Before I learned to yield?
Shatter me, great wind:
I shall possess the field.

THE PARDON
Richard Wilbur

My dog lay dead five days without a grave
In the thick of summer, hid in a clump of pine
And a jungle of grass and honeysuckle-vine.
I who had loved him while he kept alive

Went only close enough to where he was
To sniff the heavy honeysuckle-smell
Twined with another odor heavier still
And hear the flies' intolerable buzz.

Well, I was ten and very much afraid.
In my kind world the dead were out of range
And I could not forgive the sad or strange
In beast or man. My father took the spade

And buried him. Last night I saw the grass
Slowly divide (it was the same scene
But now it glowed a fierce and mortal green)
And saw the dog emerging. I confess

I felt afraid again, but still he came
In the carnal sun, clothed in a hymn of flies,

And death was breeding in his lively eyes.
I started in to cry and call his name,

Asking forgiveness of his tongueless head.
. . . I dreamt the past was never past redeeming:
But whether this was false or honest dreaming
I beg death's pardon now. And mourn the dead.

OLD HOUSE

◄§ Barry Targan

I bought a house,
an ancient house,
older than any living man,
and mended it one summer.
While the grass greened up I worked,
replaced a rotted rafter here,
there jacked up a drooping beam,
pushed in a bellying wall.
I painted my house outside and in,
hammered and nailed the creak from every floor,
made all the doors swing easy and
click shut with shaven jambs.
I routed the chipmunk, mice, and squirrel,
blocked every entering crack and chink
so animal and wind would keep their place.
I caulked, windowed, and roofed,
a summer long.
A winter, too.
And a year.
And a year and a year.

The house is older now and so am I,
and wise in houses' ways.
The paint has peeled,
the gray wood soaks in rain.
The wall has bellied out again.
Every window rattles in a storm.
Doors stick, and through the night
the house groans and fumbles at its pain.
It is old, and to complain
is age's right,
as it is to bend,
bow, settle, and rot in time.

Beam and bone twist down to dust.
Sinew and nail shrivel and rust.
No earthly mansion, flesh or wood,
lives long enough to be good.

BUSTER HILL CHASED HIS DOG

Adapted by Douglas Unger
from his novel Leaving the Land

Buster Hill brought the turkey-slaughtering industry to the small farming community of Nowell, North Dakota. He came to town ten years ago to organize Nowell-Safebuy Turkeys, a company that now produces one million turkeys a year for the national chain of Safebuy supermarkets. Buster writes the paychecks for the one thousand farmers and workers who raise, slaughter, and prepare the birds for market.

Nowell has become a one-company town; some say a one-man town. Buster Hill is the man.

One afternoon, Buster Hill reached a hand out of his front porch hammock and discovered the bulldog pup he had named Buster, after himself, was no longer there. He woke up with a start to see the dog running across the front lawn. It stopped by the curb at the front of the house and stood on its hind legs.

"Goddamnit, Buster!" Buster Hill shouted. The dog was dancing around eagerly, looking down the street. Buster Hill looked after him toward the hot dust of Main Street. A long blue Pontiac with California license plates and a woman at the wheel slowed in front of Buster's curb. The door swung open a crack, and the bulldog jumped right in.

The blue car sped off down the street with Buster Hill lumbering after it, grunting like a wounded hog. The car signaled for a left turn at the corner, turned, and signaled again, like it would double back toward Main Street. Buster Hill crossed the street, broke through the Carlsons' front gate, and cut through their yard, goring himself as he leaped over their backyard fence. He ran limping through the parking lot behind the house. The blue Pontiac made the turn, heading right through the center of Nowell toward the highway.

Buster Hill caught up to the car at the intersection. He bounced along beside the fender. He was shouting so loud that Deputy Ben Perez and a few old boys scooted off their stools at the Cove Café. They watched through the new picture window as Buster Hill went leaping sideways down the street, bouncing alongside that car like a man on a springboard. He shouted at the unknown dark-haired woman, *"That's my dog! My goddamned dog! My damned dog!"*

He was stricken. He spun around as if a sudden whirlwind had lifted him in midair and then dropped his huge body, face first, dead in the middle of Main Street.

Deputy Ben Perez hustled out of the Cove and made sure Buster Hill was dead. The blue car turned north onto the highway.

Deputy Perez ran off to wake Nowell's sheriff out of his afternoon snooze at the municipal saloon. Sheriff Meeker stood for a long time over Buster Hill's immense carcass, still red-faced and sweating. Sheriff Meeker spat, turned, and walked back across the street for the gun he had left on the hatrack at the saloon. He was still strapping the gun on, standing in the double doors of the saloon, when he stopped a minute, belted down a shot of whiskey, and tossed the glass back in to Dolores Moss. When he reached the middle of the street, he stopped again. "Dolores!" he shouted. "Dolores! Fetch me them keys!"

Dolores Moss threw his car keys out to him. The sheriff managed the rest of the distance to his brand-new black-and-tan Nowell sheriff's car. He climbed in, steadied himself, talked on the radio. He had trouble getting the new car in reverse. A small crowd scattered when the car backed nearly full circle into the street, tires smoking. Sheriff Meeker went wailing off in the wrong direction out of town.

Doc Monahan flatly refused to pronounce Buster Hill legally dead. He didn't want any part of what was coming. Sam Carlson would have him hopping with autopsy papers, official hearings, and testimony. Deputy Perez found the Doc in his office and told him the news. The Doc looked out his venetian blinds at the crowd gathering near the corpse. He asked Deputy Perez if he was sure Buster Hill was dead. "Then you go out there and don't let anybody touch a thing," he said. He waved

Deputy Perez out of his office. At his desk, Doc Monahan stuffed a pair of socks and a shaving kit into his black bag and disappeared out the back way, leaving town by back streets to avoid Sam Carlson.

It didn't take long for the news to spread. A crowd gathered in the street, standing back a good ten feet from the corpse. No one had even so much as turned Buster Hill to a more dignified position, not even Sam Carlson, the general manager and Buster Hill's second in command at the Nowell-Safebuy turkey plant. Sam Carlson raised his arms and his high woman's voice to beg the crowd: *"Please! Does anyone know what happened? Please . . . wait. . . . Is anyone willing to make a statement?"*

When he found that Doc Monahan was no longer in, Sam Carlson sent people running off for the fire department ambulance. The ambulance had gone after a case of snakebite out on the flats. No one could get Sheriff Meeker on the police radio. Sam Carlson moved through the crowd even more desperately: *"Did anyone see what happened here? Could someone please make a statement?"*

Dolores Moss at the saloon finally thought to phone the Millis Mortuary. Mr. Millis and his son took their own sweet time putting on their best black suits, polishing up their wing-tipped cowboy boots and the new maroon Cadillac hearse. Millis hoped the *Enterprise* photographer would be out there with her Polaroid, taking news photos of the scene.

Buster Hill, that man who had first brought the

turkey-slaughtering industry to Nowell, who had put this town on the map, who had managed to cut the school budget and pave the streets with cheap materials to cut his taxes—that man who had for years been the town's main source of front-page news—had become an obituary.

The crowd was growing. The slaughtering line at the Nowell-Safebuy stopped at four thousand birds. Men in bloody green aprons poured into the streets. The Pacific & Western Railroad blasted its noon whistle, calling its workers from the loading docks. The First National Bank pulled its shades.

People began to feel faint under the sun. Dolores Moss started passing out free cold beers in front of the municipal saloon. No one else seemed to know what to do. The crowd stood about, waiting for something to happen. A gleaming maroon hearse lumbered down Main Street.

The crowd pressed in. It took the strength of Mr. Millis, his son, and three turkey plant workers to heave Buster's body into the hearse. Then the hearse drove off and turned a corner, out of sight.

The people of Nowell stood solemnly in the heat, looking shocked, uprooted, not knowing whether to mourn the sudden death or feel afraid of what the future might bring, or both. It was the heat that finally moved them. The crowd began breaking up, one by one or in small groups, toward the saloon, the Cove Café, their homes—anywhere out of the blast furnace of the afternoon. They left Sam Carlson still waving his arms and calling to them from the street.

For eleven years, Sam had been Buster Hill's right-hand man, next in line for promotion. But without Buster Hill, he had no idea what he should do. The most he knew was that Safebuy's national headquarters would want some answers. He needed a statement for his superiors of just exactly what had happened.

HOW TO EAT A HOT FUDGE SUNDAE
◆§ Jonathan Holden

Start with the
clouds. Eat
the clouds. Eat through
to the ground. Eat
the ground until you tap
the first rich vein. Delve
from strata to strata
down to the cold lava
core. Stir
the lava, pick up
the whole goblet, drink
straight from the goblet
until you've finished the world.

HITTING AGAINST MIKE CUTLER

§ *Jonathan Holden*

One down. I step into the narrow,
dust-floured shooting gallery, glance
out where the tall right-hander's squint
aims in to size things up.

If it were up to him, he'd take
all afternoon, he looks so lazy—a gunslinger
who just sauntered into town, his jaw
working over a forgotten scrap of gum.

He spits, feels up the ball like a small, hard
hornet; and I hear the catcher settle
in creaking leather harness. He clucks contentedly,
does something dirty in his groin.

Far out there on the bright, bare,
heat-rippling hill, the big guy nods.
The hornet in his hand
begins to buzz.

He bows. Slowly he revolves away, then whirls,
draws. I fire back. The hornet hisses,
vanishes with a BANG, STEE-RIKE! The catcher
grins. Good chuck, good chuck, he clucks.

MY FATHER'S LOVE LETTERS

Adapted by Tess Gallagher
from her article in In Praise of What Persists

The house I grew up in overlooks the eighteen-mile stretch of water between Canada and America at its far northwest reach. Freighters, tankers, tugs, and small fishing boats pass daily, and at night, a water star, the light on a mast, marks the passing ships.

My father was a longshoreman then, and he knew the names of the ships and what they were carrying and where they came from: the *Kenyo Maru* and the *Shoshei Maru* from Japan, and the *Bright Hope* from Taiwan, carrying pulp for paper, logs for plywood, and lumber headed for California. He told me that *Maru* was a word that meant the ship would make its return home. I have been like those ships, always pointed on a return to this town of my childhood.

On Saturdays my father would drive my mother and my three brothers and me into town to shop and then to wait for him while he drank in what we called "beer joints." We would sit for hours in the car, watching the townspeople pass. In other cars there were other women and families waiting, as we were, for men in taverns.

In the life of a child these periods of stillness in parked cars were small eternities. The only amusement was to see things, and to wonder about them. Things to be seen from a parked car are not spectacular, but they were what we had. My mother was an expert at this. "See that little girl with pigtails? I bet she never had her hair cut." And sure enough, the little girl would come out twenty minutes later, her eyes red from crying, one hand in her father's and the other holding a small paper bag. "The pigtails are in there," Mother said.

Every hour or so, my mother would send me on a round of the taverns to try for a sighting of my father. I would peck on the windows and the barmaid would shake her head *no,* or motion down the dim row of faces to where my father would be sitting on his stool, forgetting, forgetting us all for a while.

My father's drinking, and the quarrels he had with my mother because of it, terrorized my childhood. There is no other way to put it. I learned then that the world was not just, that any calm was temporary, that unreasonableness could break out at any minute, thrashing aside everything and everyone in its path.

I was sixteen when I had my last lesson from the belt and my father's arm. I stood in the yard in full view of the neighbors. I looked straight ahead, without tears or cries, as a tree must look as the saw bites in. I did not feel sorry for myself during those periods of abuse, and I did not stop loving. It was our hurt not to have another way to settle things. For my father and I had no language between us in those years of my growing. Compassion, forgiveness, and strength—these were the lessons of the heart I had no choice but to learn in my childhood.

I wonder now what kept me from the easy revenge of not loving. Perhaps it was the knowledge that my parents' love was always there, although they never talked about such things. I think they didn't trust a love too easily expressed. Their love, unspoken and invisible, existed beneath the surface, rooted deep to hold during violent storms.

In those early days my father was not generally a man you could talk to. He would drive me to my piano lessons (the family's one luxury) without speaking. He smoked cigarettes one after the other. He was thinking and driving. If he had had anything to drink during these times, it was best to leave him with his thoughts. I was often afraid of him, of the violence in him, though tenderness was there too, even during his silences.

In memory now I see them, my father's work-thickened hands, my mother's back, turned in hopeless anger at the stove, where she fixed eggs for him in silence. I see my father get up from the table, show me the open palms of his hands. "Threasie," he says, "get an education. Don't get hands like these." Out of this moment and others like it I begin to understand that written and spoken words hold more than physical power, hold freedom from the slavery of hard labor, hold the power to direct and make meaning in your life.

One day I came across my father's love letters under the pillow cases in the cedar chest at the foot of my bed. The letters, written in pencil on lined tablet paper, were signed "Les" for Leslie, and following his name was a long line of XXXXX's. I would stare at those X's as though they held a clue; as though they might tell me why this man and woman had come together. The letters mainly recorded my father's days. He had worked here, was going there; he had seen so-and-so, would be coming back on such and such date. But there were also harmless jokes some workman had told him, and little teasings only my mother could have understood.

My mother's side of the correspondence was missing, probably because my father had thrown her letters away or lost them during those years he had crossed the country looking for work, riding the rails, working in the cotton fields, the oil fields, and the coal mines. My mother's letters are important to remember. They were the invisible lifeline sent out in answer to my father's heart-scrawl across the miles and days of their long courtship. But the letters are gone now, lost, except to the imagination.

My father's love letters were to be the only record that my parents had ever loved each other, for they never showed affection for one another in front of us. Years later, after I had grown up and left home, my father was to remark that they had written to each other for over ten years before they married. The fact that my mother had saved my father's love letters became a sign to me as a child that love *had* existed between them, no matter what acts might have come after.

As I write this, I begin to understand why those letters were so important to me as a child. I telephone my mother and ask her what has happened to them.

"Well, a lot of them were sent to the draft board," she says. "Your dad and I were married November of '41. Pearl Harbor hit December seventh, so they were going to draft your father. A lot of men was just jumping to get married to avoid the draft. We had to prove we had been courting. The only way was to send the letters, so they could see for themselves."

"But what happened to those letters?"

"There was only about three of them left. You kids got into them, so I burned them."

"You burned them? Why? Why'd you do that?"

"They wasn't nothing *in* them."

"But you kept them," I say. "You saved them."

"I don't know why I did," she says. "They didn't amount to anything."

I hang up. I sit on the bed and stare out the window. I think of my father's love letters being read by the members of the draft board. They believe my father's letters are a sign of long courtship. They decide not to draft him into the war. Because he wrote the letters and my mother kept them, he does not go to his death, and my birth takes place.

It is an intricate chain of events about which I had

no idea when I began to write. I think of my father's love letters burning, of how they might never have come into their true importance if I had not clung to them in my memory and returned to them here in my writing. So when I think of writing, I think of it as a courtship. I don't know if it will end in discovery, but to write is to hope for that, for the luck to discover the hidden connections.

NO

◄§ *Marnie Pomeroy*

In our world you see
no ghost or shadow:
    you think in *black* and *white*,
    you live by *don't* or *do;*

while I see only
a tricky twilight;
    I go by feel, and guess
    by afterglow.

We meet. And loving you,
I reach with all my might
    for your shining Yes
    to learn about sheer light.

But with your No
you cut me back.
    I learn how solid-black,
    how huge is night.

RAINBOWS

◄§ Marnie Pomeroy

Like this treeless town,
grim, dark, and dull,

on and on
through rain I walk.

I pass a cinder-block
gas station. There's an oil spill:

riding the black slick of rain,
it lengthens down the street.

Out comes the sun.
Struck rich, I stare

from oil rainbows
swirling at my feet

to the pure rainbow
that glows in the iris air.

NIGHT-WALKING

~§ *Marnie Pomeroy*

Snow, wind, and moon.
  Tree shadows tremble
down through the window.

I remember
  when I was younger
night-walking in winter.

Now I lament
  that all I want
is to stay in,

grown cold, and content
  just to imagine
moon-sheen, snow-shine.

THREE FABLES
◂§ William Maxwell

I. THE CARPENTER

Once upon a time there was a man of no particular age, a carpenter, whom all kinds of people entrusted with their secrets. Perhaps the smell of glue and sawdust and fresh-cut boards had something to do with it, but in any case he was not a troublemaker, and a secret is nearly always something that, if it became known, would make trouble for somebody. So they came to his shop, closed the door softly behind them, sat down on a pile of lumber, and pretended that they had come because they enjoyed watching him work. Actually, they did enjoy it. Some of them. His big square hands knew what they were doing, and all his movements were relaxed and skillful. The shavings curled up out of his plane as if the idea was to make long, beautiful shavings. He used his carpenter's rule and stubby pencil as if he were applying a moral principle. When he sawed, it seemed to have the even rhythm of his heartbeat. Though the caller might forget for five minutes what brought him here, in the end he stopped being interested in carpentry and said, "I know I can trust you, because you never repeat anything . . . ," and there it was, one more secret added to the collection, a piece of information that, if it had got out, would have broken up a friendship or caused a son to be disinherited or ruined a half-happy marriage or cost some man his job or made trouble for somebody.

The carpenter had discovered that the best way to deal with this information that must not be repeated was to forget it as quickly as possible, though sometimes the secret was so strange he could not forget it immediately, and that evening his wife would ask, "Who was in the shop today?" For people with no children have only each other to spy on, and he was an open book to her.

Sometimes the person who had confided in him seemed afterward to have no recollection of having done this, and more than once the carpenter found himself wondering if he had imagined or misremembered something that he knew perfectly well he had not imagined and would remember to his dying day. In the middle of the night, if he had a wakeful period, instead of thrashing around in the bed and disturbing his wife's sleep, he lay quietly with his eyes open in the dark and was a spectator to plays in which honorable men were obliged to tell lies, the kind and good were a prey to lechery, the old acted not merely without wisdom but without common sense, debts were repaid not in kind but in hatred, and the young rode roughshod over everybody. When he had had enough of human nature, he put all these puppets back in their box and fell into a dreamless sleep.

For many years his life was like this, but it is a mistake to assume that people never change. They don't and they do change. Without his being able to say just when it happened and whether the change was sudden or gradual, the carpenter knew that he was no longer trustworthy—that is to say, he no longer cared whether people made trouble for one another or not. His wife saw that he looked tired, that he did not always bother to stand up straight, that he was beginning to show his age. And she tried to make his life easier for him, but he was a man firmly fixed in his habits, and there was not much she could do for him except feed him well and keep small irritations from him.

Out of habit, the carpenter continued not to repeat the things people told him, but while the secret was being handed over to him he marveled that the other person had no suspicion he was making a mistake. And since the carpenter had not asked, after all, to be the repository of everybody's secret burden, it made him mildly resentful.

One day he tried an experiment. He betrayed a secret that was not very serious—partly to prove to himself that he could do such a thing and partly in the hope that word would get around that he was not to be trusted with secrets. It made a certain amount of trouble, as he knew it would, but it also had the effect of clearing the air for all concerned, and the blame never got back to him because no one could imagine his behaving in so uncharacteristic a fashion. So, after this experiment, he tried another. The butcher came in, closed the door softly, looked around for a pile of lumber to sit on, and then said, "There's something I've got to tell somebody."

"Don't tell me," the carpenter said quickly, "unless you want every Tom, Dick, and Harry to know."

The butcher paused, looked down at his terrible hands, cleared his throat, glanced around the shop, and then suddenly leaned forward and out it came.

"In short, he wanted every Tom, Dick, and Harry to know," the carpenter said to his wife afterward, when he was telling her about the butcher's visit.

"People need to make trouble the way they need to breathe," she said calmly.

"I don't need to make trouble," the carpenter said indignantly.

"I know," she said. "But you mustn't expect everyone to be like you."

The next time somebody closed the door softly and sat down and opened his mouth to speak, the carpenter beat him to it. "I know it isn't fair to tell you this," he said, "but I had to tell somebody . . ." This time he made quite a lot of trouble, but not so much that his wife couldn't deal with it, and he saw that the fear of making trouble can be worse than trouble itself.

After that, he didn't try any more experiments. What happened just happened. The candlemaker was sitting on a pile of lumber watching him saw a chestnut plank, and the carpenter said, "Yesterday the one-eyed fiddler was in here."

"Was he?" the candlemaker said; he wasn't really interested in the fiddler at that moment. There was something on his mind that he had to tell somebody, and he was waiting for the carpenter to stop sawing so he wouldn't have to raise his voice and run the risk of being overheard in the street.

"You know the blacksmith's little boy?" the carpenter said. "The second one? The one he keeps in the shop with him?"

"The apple of his eye," said the candlemaker. "Had him sorting nails when he was no bigger than a flea. Now he tends the bellows."

"That's right," said the carpenter. "Well, you know what the fiddler told me?"

"When it comes to setting everybody's feet a-dancing, there's no one like the one-eyed fiddler," the candlemaker said. "But I don't know what he'd of done without the blacksmith. Always taking him in when he didn't have a roof over his head or a penny in his pocket. Drunk or sober."

"You know what the fiddler told me? He said the blacksmith's little boy isn't his child."

"Whose is he?"

"Who does he look like?"

"Why, come to think of it, he looks like the one-eyed fiddler."

"Spitting image," the carpenter said. And not until

that moment did he realize what was happening. It was the change in the candlemaker's face that made him aware of it. First the light of an impending confidence, which had been so clear in his eyes, was dimmed. The candlemaker looked down at his hands, which were as white and soft as a woman's. Then he cleared his throat and said, "Strange nobody noticed it."

"You won't tell anybody what I told you?" the carpenter found himself saying.

"No, of course not," the candlemaker said. "I always enjoy watching you work. Is that a new plane you've got there?"

For the rest of the visit he was more friendly than usual, as if some lingering doubt had been disposed of and he could now be wholly at ease with the carpenter. After he had gone, the carpenter started to use his new plane, and it jammed. He cleaned the slot and adjusted the screw and blew on it, but it still jammed, so he put it aside, thinking the blade needed to be honed, and picked up a crosscut saw. Halfway through the plank, he stopped. The saw was not following the pencil line. He gave up and sat down on a pile of lumber. The fiddler had better clear out now and never show his face in the village again, because if the blacksmith ever found out, he'd kill him. And what about the blacksmith's wife? She had no business doing what she did, but neither did the blacksmith have any business marrying someone young enough to be his daughter. She was a slight woman with a cough, and she wouldn't last a year if she had to follow the fiddler in and out of taverns and sleep under hedgerows. And what about the little boy who so proudly tended the bellows? Each question the carpenter asked himself was worse than the one before. His head felt heavy with shame. He sighed and then sighed again, deep heavy sighs forced out of him by the weight on his heart. How could he tell his wife what he had done? And what would make her want to go on living with him when she knew? And how could he live with himself? At last he got up and untied the strings of his apron and locked the door of his shop behind him and went off down the street, looking everywhere for the one-eyed fiddler.

II. THE WOMAN WHO NEVER DREW BREATH
EXCEPT TO COMPLAIN

In a country near Finland dwelt a woman who never drew breath except to complain. There was in that country much to complain of—the long cold winters, the scarcity of food, and robber bands that descended on poor farmers at night and left their fields and barns blazing. But these things the woman had by an inequality of fate been spared. Her husband was young and strong and worked hard and was kind to her. And they had a child, a three-year-old boy, who was healthy and happy, obedient and good. The roof never leaked, there was always food in the larder and peat moss piled high outside the door for the fireplace she cooked by. But still the woman complained, morning, noon, and night.

One day when she was out feeding her hens, she heard a great beating of wings and looked up anxiously, thinking it was a hawk come to raid her hen coop, and saw a big white gander, which sailed once around the house and then settled at her feet and began to peck at the grain she had scattered for her hens. While she was wondering how she could catch the wild bird without the help of her husband, who was away in the fields, it flapped its great soft wings and said, "So far as I can see, you have less than any woman in this country to complain about."

"That's true enough," the woman said.

"Then why do you do it?" asked the bird.

"Because there is so much injustice in the world," the woman said. "In the village yesterday a woman in her sleep rolled over on her child and smothered it, and an old man starved to death last month, within three miles of here. Wherever I look, I see human misery, and here there is none, and I am afraid."

"Of what?" asked the bird.

"I am afraid lest they look down from the sky and see how blessed I am, compared to my neighbors, and decide to even things up a bit. This way, if they do look down, they will also hear me complaining, and think, 'That poor woman has lots to contend with,' and go on about their business."

"Very clever of you," the bird said, cleaning the underside of its wing with its beak. "But in the sky anything but the truth has a hollow ring. One more word of complaint out of you, and all the misfortunes of all your neighbors will be visited on you and on your husband and child." The bird flapped its wings slowly, rose above her, sailed once around the chimney, and then, flying higher and higher, was lost in the clouds. While the woman stood peering after it, the bread that she had left in the oven burned to a cinder.

The bread was the beginning of many small misfortunes, which occurred more and more frequently as time went on. The horse went lame, the hens stopped laying, and after too long a season of rain the hay all rotted in the fields. The cow went dry but produced no calf. The roof began to leak, and when the woman's husband went up to fix it, he fell and broke his leg and was laid up for months, with winter coming on. And while the woman was outside, trying to do his work for him, the child pulled a kettle of boiling water off the stove and was badly scalded.

And still no word of complaint crossed the woman's lips. In her heart she knew that worse things could happen, and in time worse things did. A day came when there was nothing to eat in the larder and the woman had to go the rounds of her neighbors and beg for food, and those she had never turned hungry from her door refused her, on the ground that anyone so continually visited by misfortune must at some time have had sexual intercourse with the Devil. The man's leg did not heal, and the child grew sickly and pale. The woman searched for edible roots and berries, and set snares for rabbits and small birds, and so kept her family from starving, until one day, when she was far away in the marshes, some drunken soldiers happened by and wantonly set fire to the barns, and went on their way, reeling and tittering. The heat of the burning barns made a downdraft, and a shower of sparks landed on the thatched roof of the farmhouse, and that, too, caught on fire. In a very few minutes, while the neighbors stood around in a big circle, not daring to come nearer because of the heat of the flames, the house burned to the ground, and the man and the child both perished. When the woman came running across the fields, crying and wringing her hands, people who had known her all their lives and were moved at last by her misfortunes tried to intercept her and lead her away, but she would have none of them. At nightfall they left her there, and she did not even see them go. She sat with her head on her knees and listened for the sound of wings.

At midnight the great bird sailed once around the blackened chimney and settled on the ground before her, its feathers rosy with the glow from the embers. The bird seemed to be waiting for her to speak, and when she said nothing it stretched its neck and arched its back and finally said, in a voice much kinder than the last time, "This is a great pity. All the misfortunes of all your neighbors have been visited on you, without a word of complaint from you to bring them on. But the gods can't be everywhere at once, you know, and sometimes they get the cart before the horse. If you'd like to complain now, you may." The wind blew a shower of sparks upward, and the bird fanned them away with its wings. The woman did not speak. "This much I can do for you," the bird said, "and I wish it was more."

When the woman raised her head, she saw a young man whose face, even in the dying firelight, she recognized. There before her stood her child, her little son, but grown now, in the pride of manhood. All power of speech left her. She put out her arms, and in that instant, brought on by such a violent beating of wings as few men have ever dreamed of, the air turned white. What the woman at first took to be tiny feathers proved to be snow. It melted against her cheek, and turned her hair white, and soon put the fire out.

The snow came down all night, and all the next day, and for many days thereafter, and was so deep that it lasted all winter, and in the spring grass grew up in what had once been the rooms of the farmhouse, but of the woman there was no trace whatever.

III. THE OLD MAN AT THE RAILROAD CROSSING

"Rejoice," said the old man at the railroad crossing, to every person who came that way. He was very old, and his life had been full of troubles, but he was still able to lower the gates when a train was expected, and raise them again when it had passed by in a whirl of dust and diminishing noise. It was just a matter of time before he would be not only old but bedridden, and so, meanwhile, people were patient with him and excused his habit of saying "Rejoice," on the ground that when you are that old not enough oxygen gets to the brain.

But it was curious how differently different people reacted to that one remark. Those who were bent on accumulating money, or entertaining dreams of power, or just busy, didn't even hear it. The watchman was somebody who was supposed to guard the railroad crossing, not to tell people how they ought to feel, and if there had been such a thing as a wooden or mechanical watchman, they would have been just as satisfied.

Those who cared about good manners were embarrassed for the poor old fellow, and thought it kinder to ignore his affliction.

And those who were really kind, but not old, and not particularly well acquainted with trouble, said "Thank you" politely, and passed on, without in the least having understood what he meant. Or perhaps it was merely that they were convinced he didn't mean anything, since he said the same thing day in and day out, regardless of the occasion or whom he said it to. "Rejoice," he said solemnly, looking into their faces. "Rejoice."

The children, of course, were not embarrassed and did not attempt to be kind. They snickered and said, "Why?" and got no answer, and so they asked another question: "Are you crazy?" And—as so often happened when they asked a question they really wanted to know the answer to—he put his hand on their heads and smiled, and they were none the wiser.

But one day a woman came along, a nice-looking woman with gray hair and lines in her face and no interest in power or money or politeness that was merely politeness and didn't come from the heart, and no desire to be kind for the sake of being kind, either, and when the old man said "Rejoice," she stopped and looked at him thoughtfully, and then she said, "I don't know what at." But not crossly. It was just a statement.

When the train had gone by and the old man had raised the gates, instead of walking on like the others, she stood there, as if she had something more to say and didn't know how to say it. Finally, she said, "This has been the worst year and a half of my entire life. I think I'm getting through it, finally. But it's been very hard."

"Rejoice," the old man said.

"Even so?" the woman asked. And then she said, "Well, perhaps you're right. I'll try. You've given me something to think about. Thank you very much." And she went on down the road.

One morning shortly after this, there was a new watchman at the crossing, a smart-looking young man who tipped his hat to those who had accumulated power or money, and bowed politely to those who valued good manners, and thanked the kind for their kindness, and to the children he said, "If you hang around my crossing, you'll wish you hadn't." So they all liked him and felt that there had been a change for the better. What had happened was that the old man couldn't get up out of bed. Though he felt just as well as before, there was no strength in his legs. So there he lay, having to be fed and shaved and turned over in bed and cared for like a baby. He lived with his daughter, who was a slatternly housekeeper and had more children than she could care for and a husband who drank and beat her, and the one thing that had made her life possible was that her old father was out of the house all day, watching the railroad crossing. So when she brought him some gruel for his breakfast that morning and he said "Rejoice," she set her mouth in a grim line and said nothing. When she brought him some more of the same gruel for his lunch, she was ready to deal with the situation. Standing over him, so that she seemed very tall, she said, "Father, I don't want to hear that word again. If you can't say anything but 'Rejoice,' don't say anything, do you hear?" And she thought he seemed to understand. But when she brought him his supper, he said it again, and in her fury she slapped him. Her own father. The tears rolled down his furrowed cheeks into his beard, and they looked at each other as they hadn't looked at each other since he was a young man and she was a little girl skipping along at his side. For a moment, her heart melted, but then she thought of how hard her life was, and that he was making it even harder by living on like this when it was time for him to die. And so she turned and went out of the room, without saying that she was sorry. And after that the old man avoided her eyes and said nothing whatever.

One day she put her head in the door and said, "There's somebody to see you."

It was the gray-haired woman. "I heard you were not feeling up to par," she said, and when the old man didn't say anything, she went on, "I made this soup for my family, and I thought you might like some. It's very nourishing." She looked around and saw that the old man's daughter had left them, so she sat down on the edge of the bed and fed the soup to him. She could tell by the way he ate it, and the way the color came into his face, that he was hungry. The dark little room looked as if it hadn't been swept in a month of Sundays, but she knew better than to start cleaning another woman's house. She contented herself with tucking the sheets in properly and straightening the covers and adjusting the pillow behind the old man's head—for which he seemed grateful, though he didn't say anything.

"Now I must go," she said. But she didn't go. Instead she looked at him and said, "Things aren't any better, they're worse. Much worse. I really don't know what I'm going to do." And when he didn't say what she expected him to say, she stopped thinking about herself and thought about him. "I don't care for the new watchman at the crossing," she said. "He stands talking to the girls when he ought to be letting the gates down, and I'm afraid some child will be run over."

But this seemed to be of no interest to him, and she quickly saw why. Death was what was on his mind, not the railroad crossing. His own death, and how to meet it. And she saw that he was feeling terribly alone.

She took his frail old hand in hers and said, "If I can just get through this day, maybe things will be better tomorrow, but in any case, I'll come to see you, to see how you are." And then, without knowing that she was going to say it but only thinking that he didn't have much longer to wait, she said what he used to say at the railroad crossing, to every person who came that way.

THE CLOUD-MOBILE

May Swenson

Above my face is a map
where continents form and fade.
Blue countries made
on a white sea are erased,
and white countries traced
on a blue sea.

It is a map that moves,
faster than real, but so slow.
Only my watching proves
that island has being,
or that bay.

It is a model of time.
Mountains are wearing away,
coasts cracking,
the ocean spills over,
then new hills heap into view
with rivercuts of blue
between them.

It is a map of change.
This is the way things are
with a stone or a star.
This is the way things go,
hard or soft, swift or slow.

ORDER OF DIET
◆§ May Swenson

1   Salt of the soil and liquor of the rock
     is all the thick land's food and mead.
     And jaws of cattle grip up
     stuffs of pasture for their bellies' need.
     We, at table with our knives,
     cut apart and swallow other lives.

2   The stone is milked to feed the tree,
     the log is killed when the flame is hungry.
     To arise in the other's body?
     Flank of the heifer we glut, we spend
     to redden our blood. Then do we send
     her vague spirit higher? Does the grain
     come to better fortune in our brain?

3   Ashes find their way to green.
     The worm is raised into the wing.
     The sluggish fish to muscle slides.
     Eventual chemistry will bring
     the lightning bug to the shrewd toad's eye.
     It is true no thing of earth can die.

4   What then feeds on us? On our blood
     and delectable flesh: the flood
     of flower to fossil, coal to snow,
     genes of glacier and volcano,
     and our diamond souls that are bent
     upward? To what Beast's intent
     are we His fodder and nourishment?

COPYRIGHT ACKNOWLEDGMENTS